To Steven
Birthday 1993
Grandma Troempler.

A WINDOW ON LIFE

A WINDOW ON LIFE

WENDELL J. ASHTON

Bookcraft
Salt Lake City, Utah

Copyright © 1985 by Bookcraft, Inc.

All rights reserved. This book or any part thereof may not be reproduced in any form whatsoever, whether by graphic, visual, electronic, filming, microfilming, tape recording or any other means, without the prior written permission of Bookcraft, Inc., except in the case of brief passages embodied in critical reviews and articles.

Library of Congress Catalog Card Number: 85-72789
ISBN 0-88494-575-8

First Printing, 1985

Printed in the United States of America

Contents

Preface

This little volume is a collection of "Viewpoint" articles written by the author as publisher of the *Deseret News*. They appeared on the back page of the *Church News* during 1984 and 1985.

They are observations of life today, with lessons from the living, both the humble and the great. There are also many messages for us now from the deeds, utterances, and writings of people who have lived on this good earth before.

There are comments on some of the significant strides of The Church of Jesus Christ of Latter-day Saints in this wondrous era.

The author expresses thanks to many who have had a hand with this book. Elder Thomas S. Monson of the Council of the Twelve, chairman of the Deseret News Publishing Company, has reviewed the articles before publication in the *Church News,* and has offered valued suggestions and encouragement. Encouragement has also come from Elder James E. Faust of the Council of the Twelve, vice-chairman of the publishing company.

Kay A. Schwendiman, another *Deseret News* associate, has been most helpful with research, as have staff members of the Church Historical Department.

Dell R. Van Orden, *Church News* editor, has ably edited the manuscripts. Enid Nelson DeBirk and Diana (Dede) H. Strong, as my administrative assistants, have not only typed the copy professionally but have given excellent suggestions.

Cory H. Maxwell, Bookcraft's editorial manager, has given valued counsel while directing the book's production. Gratitude goes to H. George Bickerstaff, Bookcraft's senior editor, for creating the book's title and for preparing the copy for book publication.

Most of all, I am indebted to my loyal companion, Belva Barlow Ashton, for doing so many jobs at home that I should have done — allowing me the time to write.

Thanks to Martin Luther

Much of the Christian world in November 1983 commemorates with grateful admiration the five hundredth anniversary of the birth in Eisleben, Germany, of Martin Luther.

He was born November 11, 1483, in the home of a humble copper miner who, through hard work and thrift, became a mining and smelting entrepreneur. That gave him the means to provide his sturdy son with deep-set eyes an education—at a time when nine of ten German people could not read.

Martin began his higher education studying law. When a lightning bolt struck near him, he vowed to pursue religion instead of law. He became both a monk and a professor of religion.

Martin Luther was a mighty man of God at a time when important events were unfolding.

Nine years after Luther's birth, Christopher Columbus, declaring his voyage heaven-directed, discovered the New World.

Two years after Luther in 1517 posted his famous Ninety-five Theses on the door of the Castle Church in Wittenberg, Ferdinand Magellan began the first around-the-world voyage.

When Luther, an obedient friar at twenty-seven, visited Rome, Michelangelo was on his back atop a scaffold, painting his masterpiece on the ceiling of the Sistine Chapel in the Vatican.

Not many years before Luther's birth, another German, Johannes Gutenberg, invented the type mold. It "made printing from movable metallic type practical for the first time."

This discovery prepared the way for the world to receive the utterances and writings of Martin Luther, the greatest of the Reformers.

Merle Severy in his commemorative article, "The World of Luther," in *National Geographic*[1] magazine writes:

"As early as 1523 Luther's tracts had romped through some 1,300 printings, perhaps a million copies. From 1516 to 1546 he averaged a treatise every two weeks—writing enough to fill 102 huge volumes of the famous Weimar edition, making him the most prolific religious figure in history, as well as the most written about since Christ."

Among Luther's notable contributions was his placing "the Bible in the hands of the common people, in the language of their every day speech."

His translation of the Bible into German has been described as "a literary masterpiece." More than any other, it has been said, he created the modern German language.

He wished that "all my books would disappear and the Holy Scriptures alone be read."

He gave the European a new concept of himself—that he had access to God without intercession of clergy.

Luther spoke out against indulgences, through which church members of his day were told they could purchase forgiveness.

He opposed clerical celibacy, took himself a bride, and "elevated wifely status from housekeeper to helpmate."

This former choir boy, who played both the flute and lute, wrote music brilliantly. His best known hymn, "A Mighty Fortress Is Our God," for which he wrote both the lyrics and music, appears in our Latter-day Saint hymnal.

He stressed congregational singing as an important part of worship.

After his daughter Magdalene, thirteen, died in his arms he said tenderly:

"Darling Lena, it is well with you. You will rise and shine like a star, yes, like the sun."

Members of The Church of Jesus Christ of Latter-day Saints during this Martin Luther five hundredth anniversary year have so much for which to thank God for him.

Luther more than any other brought the Reformation. It opened the way for the restoration of the fullness of the gospel of Jesus Christ.

And through that restored gospel all mankind in today's challenging, changing world can know the true meaning of "A Mighty Fortress Is Our God."

Notes

1. Oct. 1983.

Trust at Home

Writing for the Minneapolis *Star and Tribune,* Nancy Danielson foresees home life in the western world in 1990.

By then, she says, the "electronic homestead" will be here.

No longer will many of us need ride the bus or drive the car to work. From our home in a high rise or hidden in the woods on a hill we shall be telecommuting to our business contacts. Home computers and telephone lines, plus other wondrously developing tools, will do the job.

At home we'll do our banking, buying, bartering, and other business.

Indeed we are entering what Utah-reared John Naisbitt, in his best-selling *Megatrends,* calls the Information Age.

In many ways, the home is returning to where it was before the Industrial Revolution of the 1700s and 1800s. Then, most manufacturing was done in rural cottages.

That was the boyhood world of a spidery little English hunchback who often wore three pair of stockings and wrapped himself in flannels. He was Alexander Pope. In his *Essay on Man* in the 1730s he wrote:

"An honest man's the noblest work of God."

Parents in the Information Age will no doubt spend more of their time at home, as they did in Pope's day. Children and grandchildren will be there. Watching.

And the moves they watch in the home may be global, thanks to satellites and other electronics.

What will the business executive do who today tells his secretary at the office to advise callers, except for a chosen few, that he is "out" when he does not want to be disturbed?

What will he do if he is inclined to cheat a little on a bid or an expense account, when he is operating at home? How will the plumber do business at home—the plumber who tells a customer the price for the job is $100 by check or $75 by cash, to avoid reporting income for taxes?

Will the code in the electronic home be that which, unfortunately, has become too common in the marketplace:

Fudging is all right if you do not get caught. It might even be more profitable.

The Royal Bank of Canada already this young year has distributed widely a newsletter titled "The Sense of Morality."

The article cites two examples of the growing lack of integrity in a world entering the Information Age:

1. A racing car driver had been disqualified for breaking a rule to win a championship. He appealed the ruling on grounds that his dishonesty was "common practice."

2. A student sued her university for refusing to grant her a degree because she was caught cheating on her final exams.

The newsletter makes the point that strict honesty in its truest sense is caring selflessness.

Immanuel Kant, the brilliant German thinker who lived during the unfolding Industrial Revolution, urged us to treat people "in every case as an end, never as a means."

Treating others as a means too often leads to taking advantage, dishonest dealings.

The Lord said it even better to Moses:

"Thou shalt not defraud thy neighbour. . . . Love thy neighbour as thyself." (Leviticus 19:13, 18.)

At a recent family gathering on his deceased father's hundredth birthday anniversary, a member of the Quorum of the Twelve distributed to all children, grandchildren, and great grandchildren present a transparent paperweight containing a silver Eisenhower dollar. Inscribed over the dollar was the name of the Apostle's father. Under the dollar were the birthdate and hundredth anniversary date. Etched in larger type at the bottom was:

"Man of Integrity"

No legacy is richer than an honest name.

As the world moves toward the "electronic homestead," how increasingly important is pure integrity. There is nothing like it for genuine joy. And, in the Information Age, is it not true as always:

"Men are that they might have joy." (2 Nephi 2:25.)

Turning
the Key

"Thou shalt love thy neighbour as thyself." (Matthew 19:19.)

That is one of the elegant lines of all literature. More important, the Lord has proclaimed it the second greatest commandment.

Jehovah gave that joy-bringing edict through Moses to the children of Israel in the wilderness, over fourteen centuries before the birth of the Prince of Peace in Bethlehem. (Leviticus 19:18.)

Jesus repeated the commandment to the rich young ruler in Perea.

Again, He exalted the line in answering an inquiring Pharisee lawyer.

The Relief Society of The Church of Jesus Christ of Latter-day Saints continues to quietly, but eloquently, implement that divine law with both group and individual action.

In Tempe, Arizona, for weeks now a ward Relief Society has been taking turns driving a woman, crippled by arthritic legs, daily to a hospital for therapy.

Recently a Dallas singles ward Relief Society moved into action upon learning of a divorcee member's near-death blood clot. For two weeks the young women did her housework, laundry, and meal making, and caringly comforted her.

For over five years, a ward Relief Society presidency in Salt Lake Valley has delivered a homemade poppyseed cake to every woman in the ward on her birthday anniversary.

In Idaho's Twin Falls area, a group of Relief Society widows in a ward began making quilts together. Out of the activity developed a "kitchen band" that warmed hearts and cheered gatherings with their music from harmonicas, drums, violins, and other instruments.

From Santiago to Stockholm and from Seoul in Korea to Seville in Spain, Relief Society sisters are there with food and helping hands when death, illness, or distress occur.

In groups they serve happily in canning grapefruit, beef, chicken, tomatoes, peas, and other produce for Church welfare storehouses.

Some 510,000 of the approximately 1.6 million Relief Society members meet each week in about fourteen thousand ward and branch meetings.

In eighty-nine countries and sixteen territories, together they study lessons on Spiritual Living, with such subjects as "Joy through Repentance" and "The Power of Faith." They also discuss topics under Mother Education—such as how to praise children and build self-esteem. There are Social Relations lessons, and others on Cultural Refinement. Women discuss fabrics, home design, how to handle wills, buy food and clothes, plan financial security, and deal with insurance.

They learn how to store and use grain in time of need, including how to sprout it for salad greens.

They discuss Compassionate Service lessons.

Hundreds of thousands of them, including the prophet's wife, each month visit assigned homes with cheering messages.

All of this activity began 142 years ago in the upper room of Joseph Smith's brick store in bustling Nauvoo, Illinois, on the Mississippi River. It was Thursday afternoon, March 17, 1842. John Tyler was president of the United States, and some hundred miles to the southeast of Nauvoo, in Springfield, Abraham Lincoln at thirty-three was still single, serving his fourth term in the Illinois Legislature.

Hundreds of Church converts from Britain, coming up the Mississippi in paddle-wheel steamers, were arriving in Nauvoo. Red brick homes were abuilding, shops were expanding, and the off-white stone walls of a temple were rising.

Meeting with eighteen women in that room over the store, the thirty-six-year-old Prophet established the Relief Society when women's organizations were virtually unknown.

Declared Joseph Smith:

"I now turn the key in your behalf in the name of the Lord, and this Society shall rejoice, and knowledge and intelligence shall flow down from this time henceforth; this is the beginning of better days for the poor and the needy, who shall be made to rejoice and pour forth blessings on your head."

Thus was created a Society to ennoble women, broaden and enrich their horizons, to bring them together for better serving their neighbors—as Jehovah taught ancient Israel and Jesus the multitudes in His time.

Barbara B. Smith, serving in her tenth year as general president of the Relief Society said:

"The Relief Society brings Latter-day Saint women together —women of diverse interests and backgrounds and situations— to grow together in a glorious sisterhood."

Giving That
Is Golden

If there is an "Unknown Soldier" among the mighty prophets of
the Old Testament it is Malachi.

Little, if anything, is known of his life.

He gave us the Old Testament's last book, written approximately 430 B.C. There are only four short chapters. But in them
Malachi foretells of John the Baptist and the earthly mission of
the Messiah. Malachi also speaks of Elijah's restoring role in
turning hearts, and of the glorious Second Coming.

Malachi, too, speaks tellingly of tithing:

"Bring ye all the tithes into the storehouse, that there may be
meat in mine house, and prove me now herewith, saith the Lord
of hosts, if I will not open you the windows of heaven, and pour
you out a blessing, that there shall not be room enough to receive
it." (Malachi 3:10.)

What are the blessings that fall from the windows of heaven
through tithe paying?

One of them is the repeated lesson in giving generously and
quietly to a noble cause and the glowing inner joy that comes
through that kind of giving.

George Bernard Shaw, the Dublin-born playwright and essayist, wrote of strength that comes through being involved in a cause bigger than yourself.

Through paying a full tithe, one becomes quietly but powerfully involved in the greatest cause on earth: the kingdom of God.

Another blessing from heaven's windows to the tithe payer is the unmatched teaching in integrity—honesty with oneself and his Maker when no one is watching.

John Foster Bennett was a pioneer Utah industrialist and father of Wallace F. Bennett, former U.S. senator, and Harold F. Bennett, for many years chief executive officer of ZCMI.

John's father, Richard, worked in a hairpin factory in Birmingham, England, the city where John was born.

When John was only a tot, his mother, Maria, and her family joined the Church. Her husband Richard did not join, but he accompanied his wife and family to Utah. In Utah, Brigham Young assigned him to maintain machinery in a sawmill in Salt Lake Valley.

His son John left school at twelve years of age to help his parents eke out a livelihood. His job at the time was, in part, leading two blind men carrying stone chiseling tools to a sharpening wheel on City Creek. He was paid twenty-five cents a week in tithing scrip.

John, who was called "Bob," one day was confronted by his father. The father said:

"Bob, have you been to the circus?"

"No," Bob answered.

"Why?" said the father.

"Because, Dad, I didn't have the money."

Father: "Then why didn't you sneak in like the rest of the kids?"

Bob: "Because that isn't what you taught me, Dad."

The same conversation was repeated regarding Bob's not attending shows in the ward hall.

Then the father said: "Well, Bob, you must pay an admission price to get in. Likewise, there is an admission price into that Church you have joined. It's 10 percent of your earnings. Bob, pay the admission price. Be honest. You don't get anything for nothing."

Bob paid his tithing on the $16 he had saved in scrip from the old tithing house.

At tithing settlement time for years afterward, Richard Bennett would ask his son: "Bob, have you paid your full tithing? Have you paid the admission price?"

John F. Bennett paid an honest tithe until his death in 1938 at seventy-two, honored as one of Utah's leading businessmen and for nearly three decades general treasurer of the Sunday School of the Church.

Tithing is a great teacher. It is also a law of the Lord. Abraham paid his tithes to Melchizedek. Young Jacob, even before marriage, vowed to pay his tenth to the Lord. Tithing was paid in the Savior's day. Through the Prophet Joseph Smith the Lord commanded His people to pay a tenth of their annual interest or income. (See D&C 119:4.)

"The law of tithing is a test by which the people as individuals shall be proved," wrote President Joseph F. Smith.

Indeed, tithing, as promised by the Lord to Malachi, is giving that is golden.

Sodom with Wings

Kari Kirk Harrington, a former cheerleader, at twenty-three is an attractive blond mother of one, with another on the way.

Her husband is a CPA. They reside in Indianapolis, Indiana, known worldwide for its annual Memorial Day 500 automobile race (over 300,000 spectators). Indianapolis is sometimes called "Crossroads of America."

Kari not long ago attended a special family-oriented conference on community values in Cincinnati, Ohio.

There were discussions on the growing plague of pornography. National leaders spoke movingly on the subject. But what touched Kari more than anything was the showing of a videotape described as the most in demand at a Cincinnati suburb store.

Kari was shocked.

Returning to Indianapolis, she moved into action.

In her neighborhood she visited six drugstores and convenience outlets. She checked each to learn if it was selling sex explicit literature. Kari found three of the stores did not. To each manager she wrote a personal letter of commendation and appreciation.

She found a drugstore selling the seamy literature. Kari sought out the woman manager. The manager referred her to the drugstore owner. For three days Kari tried to reach him by phone.

Then she got him. She asked him if he believed in promoting promiscuity. He replied that he was a family man.

Kari continued: "I have spent sixteen dollars in your drugstore on prescriptions the past three weeks. I'm not going to spend another penny in your drugstore as long as you sell that smut. Furthermore, I'm going to tell my physician, whose prescriptions brought me to your drugstore, what you are selling."

About an hour later, she received a phone call from the woman drugstore manager. She said: "Our owner has asked me to tell you that we are removing all the smut magazines from our drugstore and from his other two drugstores too."

A determined young mother made a big difference in her neighborhood.

Thousands of other concerned Americans are joining the fight against the menace of obscenity. They are writing their Congressmen to pull out of a House committee a bill that would put more teeth in enforcement of the nation's anti-obscenity laws. They are appealing to the U.S. Justice Department to "take off the gloves" with "porn peddlers."

Concerned Americans are moving against pornography on videotapes and cable TV. They are letting advertisers who help sponsor raunchy television programs know that they will not buy their products.

In many areas, Latter-day Saints are at the forefront. They are working through such organizations as Morality in Media, Citizens for Decency Through Law, Action Group on Media Pornography, National Federation for Decency, and Citizens Concerned for Community Values.

The battle against pornography grows in other nations too. A few weeks ago more than 750 people paid $35 each to attend in Toronto a 10½-hour symposium on media violence and pornography.

Canadians, who receive 85 percent of their television programming from the United States, are concerned about the smut and violence lacing much of what wings across the border.

If there is truly an "ugly American," he could well be the purveyor of pornography.

Consider these facts:

• Americans spend approximately $7 billion a year for pornography.

• There are approximately 750 pornography motion picture houses in the nation, not including those showing pornographic homosexual movies exclusively.

• Crime-spawning obscenity is now entering American homes through cable TV.

Nearly ten years ago President Spencer W. Kimball, in general conference (October 4, 1974), spoke out powerfully:

"There is a link between pornography and the low, sexual drives and perversions. . . . How low can humans plunge! . . . Murder, robbery, rape, prostitution are fed on this immorality. . . . We are shocked at the depths to which many people go to assert their freedom."

Sodom and Gomorrah nearly four thousand years ago were destroyed by the Lord for their wickedness, including fornication and homosexuality. But in those twin cities of sin the abominations were confined to the local area, probably just south of the Dead Sea. Sodom and Gomorrah could not have had worse obscenity that we now hear all too frequently. But today's takes wings, through the wonders of satellites and television and videotape and the vivid colors of the printed page.

The same wings that carry the uplift of a symphony, a great and good play, the Olympics, or most importantly, the message of the Messiah—these same wings can and do carry the sordid to the hearth of tens of millions of homes.

That is a mighty challenge in this dawning of the Information Age.

This is a time to fight back, to protect the moral sinew of the land.

This is a time to be concerned and act—like a twenty-three-year-old blond mother in Indianapolis.

Planting Time

April is planting time in much of the western world.

In Utah it is the season when the rich, brown loam in the high mountain valleys receives seeds of many kinds. It is a time when yellow dogtooth violets start appearing on the hillsides.

In Utah it is planting time, too, for the Church.

This spring there will be sowing before the towering gold-tinted organ pipes under the expansive oval roof of the Tabernacle on Temple Square. It is general conference time.

Messages from the walnut-hewn pulpit will be carried by satellite 22,300 miles above the earth to some 650 assembled congregations. Hundreds of thousands more will see and hear by television and radio.

The dominant figure in all this may not even be there. Time's infirming hand has touched tenderly the stocky, durable frame of Spencer Woolley Kimball.

But the power of this doggedly dedicated prophet of the living Lord will be felt abundantly.

Consider the planting President Kimball did just ten years ago. It was his first major address as the new president of the Church.

He spoke early that Thursday morning on April 4, 1974, at a temporary pulpit on the stage of the auditorium in the Church Office Building. Seated on the yellow cushioned seats before him were General Authorities, regional representatives, auxiliary leaders, and a few others. It was the opening meeting of the annual regional representatives seminar.

President Kimball's address, over an hour long, was one of the great declarations by a leader of the Church in this century.

As President Kimball spoke, on the other side of the wall of the auditorium's foyer — on the massive east wall of the building's lobby — a painter was at work. He toiled behind a high plywood barricade. He was handsome, brown-haired, fortyish Grant Romney Clawson. He was reproducing in oils a painting, approximately sixteen by four feet, by a master illustrator of the Savior's life — kindly, baldish, and bushy-browed Harry Anderson of Ridgefield, Connecticut.

The oil's subject: The resurrected Jesus, immediately prior to His ascension, giving His charge to the Eleven outside the walls of Jerusalem, "Go ye therefore, and teach all nations, baptizing them in the name of the Father, and of the Son, and of the Holy Ghost." (Matthew 28:19.)

The mural, commissioned by President Kimball's predecessor, President Harold B. Lee, gloriously portrays the "planting time" message.

Here are some of the seeds and the fruits:

President Kimball said: "I wonder if we are doing all we can. Are we complacent in our approach to teaching all the world? We have been proselyting now 144 years. Are we prepared to lengthen our stride? Enlarge our vision?

". . . I think of the numerous nations that are still untouched. . . .

". . . I feel that when we have done all in our power that the Lord will find a way to open doors. . . .

"Is anything too hard for the Lord?"

Since that talk in April 1974, the number of Church members has grown from 3,385,909 to 5,300,000; stakes, from 675 to 1,465; missions, from 113 to 177. The number of full-time missionaries then was 17,564. Now, it is 26,844.

Stakes and wards or missions or branches have been established under his presidency in countries like Greece, Malaysia, Jamaica, Nigeria, Ghana, New Guinea, Haiti, Dominican Republic, Sri Lanka, and other nations new to Church congregations.

In President Kimball's past ten years as prophet-leader, the Book of Mormon has been translated into forty-six additional languages.

But the more important fruits of President Kimball's leadership are in the lives of individuals—those who have discovered the joy of living the restored gospel of the Master.

Yes, seeds are sown by the Lord's oracles at General Conference. How these thought seeds root and grow will depend in a large measure on the hearts of those who hear.

At planting time it is good to contemplate that a tiny seed only one-sixteenth inch long can become a towering redwood, one of the tallest living things.

Father of Mischief

Slender, shy, almost-silent Calvin Coolidge in 1927, as president of the United States, spoke before a hushed Congress on the 195th anniversary of the birth of George Washington.

Said President Coolidge of his nation's first president:

"His stature increases with the increasing years. In wisdom of action, in purity of character, he stands alone. We cannot yet estimate him. We can only indicate our reverence for him and thank the Divine Providence which sent him to serve and inspire his fellow men."

George Washington was a man's man.

At forty-three he was described as broad-shouldered, six feet, two inches tall, two hundred pounds, wearing size thirteen shoes, massive hands, blue eyes, with brown hair usually well-powdered. He liked hunting ducks and wild turkeys, fishing—also the theater and dance.

He loved horses. Two days before his death at sixty-seven, he was on his horse five hours.

Sixteen years earlier, Washington, from his headquarters as commander in chief of the American army in Newburgh, New York, wrote a letter to his nephew, Bushrod Washington.

General Washington had just defeated Lord Cornwallis at Yorktown. The Treaty of Paris, officially ending the Revolutionary War, was only a few months away.

Bushrod was studying law in Philadelphia. He later became a justice in the Supreme Court. Washington willed most of his papers to Bushrod.

General Washington in that letter to his nephew wrote about making friendships.

"Be courteous to all, but intimate with few, and let those few be well tried before you give them your confidence."

The general wrote him to "feel for the afflictions and distresses of every one."

He counseled the law student to dress plainly but genteelly.

Then, Washington concluded with far more words than on any other subject in the letter. He said it "is of first importance."

The subject? Gambling.

Penned Washington: "It is the child of avarice, the brother of inequity, and father of mischief. It has been the ruin of many worthy families. . . . The losing gamester, in hopes of retrieving past misfortunes, goes on from bad to worse."

He concluded by terming gambling "an abominable practice."

America, and all the world, could well read today that letter of a caring uncle to a nephew of promise.

Consider these facts compiled by *U.S. News and World Report* in a full-scale account on gambling in the United States:

Americans bet more than $1 trillion a year, equal to $4,500 for every man, woman, and child.

Legal betting on horses alone exceeds $7 billion a year.

Only four states—Mississippi, Indiana, Utah, and Hawaii—still prohibit all forms of gambling.

The article notes that many churches, which have in decades past crusaded against gambling, have prostituted themselves. In forty-two states, churches and other nonprofit organizations "usually have the sole right to sponsor bingo for cash prizes."

Washington said gambling is the "father of mischief." FBI crime figures agree:

Las Vegas, "gaming capital of the world," in 1983 had a crime index total of 17,096. That compares with 13,828 in Albuquerque, which has more than twice the population. Las Vegas last year had 45 murders; Salt Lake City, with the approximate same corporate population, had 7. Las Vegas had 998 reported robberies; Salt Lake City, 342.

"For tens of thousands of Americans, gambling is an addiction as powerful as alcoholism or drug abuse," concludes *U.S. News and World Report.* The magazine follows with a first-person report of a reformed compulsive gambler, a forty-one-year-old New York City suburb store owner. He summarizes:

"You never really come out ahead in gambling. Even when you win, you still lose because you always want to parlay the money into a bigger win—and then you lose it all."

For cities and states considering legalized gambling on horse racing and other gaming forms, Twentieth Century Fund, a New York research group, has a message, after a study of legalized betting:

"Gambling's get-rich-quick appeal appears to mock capitalism's core values: disciplined work habits, thrift, prudence, adherence to routine, and the relationship between effort and reward."

George Washington was right about a lot of things.

Gambling was certainly one.

Divine Momentum

In the cool, fresh Colombian air of Bogota, "the Athens of America," thousands of Latter-day Saints are talking joyously about a new temple that will soon be constructed there.

Similar rejoicing about new temples throbs in Toronto, monarch among Canada's cities—and in San Diego, California; Las Vegas, Nevada; and Portland, Oregon.

Heart surgeons in the People's Republic of China (where he has conducted surgery seminars), in Argentina (where he has received the Republic's Gold Medal), across Europe and in other continents, and throughout the United States and Canada—will take note admiringly of the call to the Council of the Twelve of Dr. Russell M. Nelson, internationally acclaimed thoracic surgeon.

Leading educators, jurists, and public television executives in America and abroad have been or will be stirred with the call of an associate they esteem, Dr. Dallin H. Oaks, to the Twelve.

In America and beyond, men and women who have served with or under six able and dedicated Church leaders are applauding their calls to the First Quorum of the Seventy. They include:

John K. Carmack, Russell C. Taylor, Robert B. Harbertson, Devere Harris, Spencer H. Osborn, and Philip T. Sonntag.

Women of the Church around the world are voicing their gratitude this week to Barbara Bradshaw Smith, completing nearly a decade as general president of the Relief Society, and her counselors and board.

Lives in many nations have been lifted by the heartfelt eloquence and caring touch of Elaine Anderson Cannon and her counselors in the Young Women's general presidency. They now move on to new Church responsibilities after some six years of Churchwide leadership with a dedicated and distinguished board.

In southern Alberta, where the fields turn gold with rippling grain and the pink wild roses grow, there is pride this week in the new honor coming to Ardeth Greene Kapp, who as a brown-eyed, black-haired girl grew up there. She is the new Young Women's general president.

Women of the Church who have been blessed by her leadership in her stake, the mission field, as both a Relief Society and YMMIA general board member, and as national president of an LDS college women's sorority are expressing joy in the appointment of Barbara Woodhead Winder as new general president of the Relief Society.

All this global outpouring comes from activities and messages at the 154th annual general conference of the Church in the historic Salt Lake Tabernacle.

The conference was a powerful expression of divine momentum, that the restored kingdom of God on earth—"the stone . . . cut out of the mountain without hands" described by Daniel (Daniel 2:45)—is rolling forth mightily.

President Spencer W. Kimball was at three general sessions of the conference. He is restrained, as is his First Counselor in the First Presidency, President Marion G. Romney, with age's physical infirmities. Yet there was evidence everywhere of a church of vigor and strength and upward thrust, that the Lord directs His Church.

Consider these conference messages:

President Ezra Taft Benson noted that when he and President Kimball were ordained Apostles just over forty years ago there were 146 stakes—and less than a million Church members. Today there are 1,460 stakes—ten times as many—and Church membership exceeds 5.4 million, President Benson said.

President Gordon B. Hinckley reported there are now under construction 896 Church buildings, most of them meetinghouses, around the world. Church congregations are now meeting in ninety nations, more than ever before.

President Hinckley said there were five thousand copies in the first edition of the Book of Mormon in 1830. Today editions of a million are rolling off the presses yearly. This sacred scripture is now printed in sixty-seven languages, he said.

The moving addresses of four women leaders at the conference were testaments of the exalting role of the Church with the daughters of Eve.

There were fervent calls for more missionaries to carry the Savior's restored gospel to expanding areas of this planet, to bring the miracle of conversion to increasing thousands.

Divine momentum in a growing Church indeed was there at conference.

The challenge to each Church member now is to instill and retain that joyous momentum for righteousness in his or her own soul—in a permissive, wayward world.

Morning of Joy

It was early springtime in sun-showered Mesa, founded in the flowering Arizona desert near Phoenix ninety-seven years before by the Mormons.

Now in 1975, Mesa, growing like a gourd, was witnessing the first opening to the public of a temple of The Church of Jesus Christ of Latter-day Saints following its remodeling.

The glistening white, terra-cotta, colonnaded Arizona Temple, completed in 1927, had just undergone extensive interior restructuring. Now it was open for public tours prior to rededication by President Spencer W. Kimball.

Among the early visitors was a group of Arizona clergymen. Following their tour, they assembled in a temple room for questions. Assigned to host them was Elder Gordon B. Hinckley of the Council of the Twelve.

One of the clergymen asked:

"Tell us, please. Why do we see no crosses in this beautiful building?"

Elder Hinckley's response:

"I do not wish to give offense to any of my Christian brethren who use the cross. . . . But for us the cross is the symbol of the dying Christ, while our message is a declaration of the living Christ. The lives of our people are the symbol of our worship."

Indeed, Latter-day Saints, as symbols of the reality and meaning of that first Easter, should radiate more joy than any other people on earth.

They, through the restored gospel of the Redeemer, know that through Christ every person who has lived or will live on earth will receive a literal resurrection. Each will have his or her body and spirit reunited "in resurrected immortality."

They know that Jesus also opened the way for the righteous to receive additionally "the greatest of all the gifts of God"— eternal life.

What a wondrous morning that first Easter was!

A small group of sorrowing women, carrying spices and ointments for embalming, moved at dawn toward the sepulcher where the body of Jesus had been laid three days before.

Among them was Mary of Magdala.

She became the first earthly witness of the resurrection, as she met her risen Lord in the sepulcher garden.

"One word from His living lips changed her agonized grief to ecstatic joy," wrote James E. Talmage in *Jesus the Christ.*

Jesus said to her: "Mary."

Mary of Magdala was never the same after that "morning of joy."

Around the world "mornings of joy" come to approximately two-hundred thousand new converts to the restored church of the Redeemer every year. Generally they are young—some 70 percent of them twenty-eight years old or younger.

One of them was a young adult who came to the doorstep of the Church mission home on New York City's Fifth Avenue.

It was Easter, 1973.

He was shabbily dressed with a faded, wrinkled, brown sport shirt. His disheveled black hair reached almost to his shoulders.

He had been to the museum across the street. There, he was impressed with the pre-Columbian artifacts from the Americas.

To the short, sixtyish Church man who met him at the door, he said: "I'm impressed with the intelligence of those ancient peoples. I understand you Mormons know something of them. Will you tell me?"

The Book of Mormon was briefly explained. The caller was introduced to the full-time missionaries.

The swarthy fellow had trouble with the miracles surrounding the book. He did not believe in God.

In his Manhattan room he tried a prayer. He asked for no visions, no angels.

"But if you are there, God, and these things are true, give me an assurance."

It came.

He had his own "morning of joy."

Less than a decade later, the same young adult was Bishop Robert J. Spanvill of the Manhattan Second Ward, looking in pin stripes like the New York computer executive he was.

The miracle of the "morning of joy" continues to repeat.

Time of Testing

He was only sixteen, big of body and quick and mature of mind. He was a farm boy from Potsdam, in northeastern New York state, some twenty-five miles from the Canadian border.

Near-sighted and weakly as a lad, he had been taunted and bullied at school. He had resolved to gain respect, to whip "every boy of his size and age" at school—which as a teen he did.

His name was George A. (for Albert) Smith.

Now, for just over a year, George and his family had been in Kirtland, Ohio, headquarters of the four-year-old Church, presided over by his cousin, Joseph Smith.

The year was 1834, and rough-hewn Andrew Jackson, born in a Carolina log cabin, was president of the United States.

A call went out from the Prophet Joseph Smith for the able-bodied men of the fledgling Church to gather in Kirtland and march as a frontier army nearly a thousand miles to western Missouri. There they were to bring help to the distressed members of the Church. Hundreds of them had been plundered and driven from their homes.

The army became known as Zion's Camp.

Among those who enlisted was young George A. Smith.

Zion's Camp was organized in the spring of 1834 with the Prophet Joseph Smith assuming command May 5 that year. The Prophet was twenty-nine, about the average age of the some 105 original volunteers. However, one of them, Samuel Baker, from Norton, Ohio, was "nearly eighty."

This was a time of testing.

Brigham Young had been married to Mary Ann Angell just six days when the call to enlist was sounded. His first wife had died, leaving two little daughters. Brigham was one of the first to enlist.

Other men, with little or no money, volunteered. Stalwart women remained behind.

George A. Smith's parents fitted him out with a musket, a pair of pantaloons made of bed ticking, several cotton shirts, a straw hat, coat and vest, a blanket, and a new pair of boots. Most of his belongings he carried in a heavy cloth knapsack.

After the first day of marching (twenty-seven miles), his new boots had blistered his feet severely. The Prophet Joseph gave George a pair of his boots, much more comfortable.

The march had its trials. At times George's stockings were wet with blood. Deep mud required pulling wagons with ropes. Sometimes the only water to drink was in miry sloughs, and George "learned to strain wigglers with my teeth." On a hot, dry day near the Grand River, a thunderstorm brought precious water, with thirsty trekkers drinking from horse tracks.

Rattlesnakes were found under and in blankets.

In his diary, the youth wrote of "poor quality of bread, bad corn dodger, frowsy butter, strong honey, maggoty bacon and cheese."

Cholera took a few of Zion's Camp, which grew on the trail to 207 men, 11 women, and 11 children—with 25 baggage wagons.

There were murmurings.

George A. Smith for much of the journey slept in Joseph Smith's tent "directly at his feet." The youth heard the Prophet counsel with leaders, transgressors, and complainers. George saw the Prophet reprove the cook for serving him sweet bread while others received sour bread. He wanted no favors.

As the forty-five-day march drew to an end, the young

trekker wrote of his prophet-leader: "But during the entire trip he never uttered a murmur of complaint."

Some apostatized.

Zion's Camp indeed was a time of testing.

From its faithful were drawn members of the first Council of the Twelve, organized the following winter (February 14, 1835).

Four years later, at twenty-one, George A. Smith in Far West, Missouri, was ordained an Apostle, the youngest ever so called in this dispensation. At fifty-one he was sustained First Counselor in the First Presidency. He died at fifty-eight.

He was a mighty colonizer. St. George, Utah, is named for him. He was a gifted writer, speaker, lawyer, historian, educator, and statesman.

Zion's Camp was a testing time for George A. Smith, and for many others.

Each of us has his or her own testing times: illness or death of a loved one, rejections in love, financial reverses, failure in a pursuit, times of temptation, disappointments by kith or kin, wealth or station, acclaim.

Of Zion's Camp, young George A. Smith wrote in his journal: "The journey was long and tedious temporally speaking." Then he added that it indeed was an experience "according to the mind and will of the Lord."

11

They Are Mothers, Too

This was ancient Egypt. Some historians say the year was 1571 B.C.

The kingdom along the fertile Nile already was venerable in power and glory. The great pyramids had been there nearly a thousand years. For well over a century now the children of Israel had been living in Egypt.

In this year, "a goodly child" was born in Egypt to a Levite couple—when there was a decree from the pharaoh that every male born among the Hebrews be "cast into the river."

For three months the Levite mother hid her child. Then she made for him an ark of bulrushes, daubed with slime and pitch. The babe was put in the floating basket, placed among the flags on the river's edge.

When the pharaoh's daughter came with her maidens to the river to bathe, she saw the ark amid the flags. Opening the basket, the princess beheld the babe. The child cried, and the princess "had compassion on him."

Meanwhile, the babe's sister had "stood afar off," watching. She stepped forth, and asked the princess if she would like a

Hebrew nurse for the infant. The princess agreed, and the child's mother responded as the nurse.

The pharaoh's daughter took the babe as her own. She named him Moses "because I drew him out of the water." (See Exodus 2.)

For some precious, watchful hours at the water's edge the sister of the baby Moses served as his mother—at a crucial time in the great prophet-leader's life.

Some 3,417 years later, in a floorless log hut on the banks of the Missouri River, another older sister assumed a mother's role.

She was Ellen Spencer, just turned fourteen. Her mother, Catherine Curtis Spencer, had died as the family crossed Iowa with the Mormon pioneers earlier in the year. Now Ellen's father, Orson Spencer, was called on a Church mission to Great Britain. (Orson Spencer later became the first chancellor of the University of Deseret, later Utah.)

This was a cold, cruel place called Winter Quarters late in 1846. Little Ellen Spencer became head of the household of six children. Through two winters on the Missouri, Ellen mothered the brood—also across the plains and through another bitter winter in Salt Lake Valley, first in a log, then an adobe abode.

No crown glistens more than that of noble motherhood.

John A. Shedd, the American educator, said:

"Simply having children does not make mothers."

Nor does one need bear children to earn the crown of motherhood.

On Mother's Day, surely honor should come, too, to the queenly "other mothers"—like the Levite sister of the infant Moses, pioneer Ellen Spencer, motherly aunts, adopting mothers, caring stepmothers, childless wives, and women who are single through circumstances beyond their control who nobly play the mother role.

Recently at a Latter-day Saint funeral, thirtyish Becky Priscilla Lees, high school English teacher, paid tribute to a great aunt (Becky Almond), never married:

"Each of us took left turns in our lives, but . . . right ones were taken because of your influence. . . .

"Two generations say 'thank you' for being a mother, guardian angel, and best friend."

Never has the need for mothering been greater than during this second half of the twentieth century, when women's roles have changed so much. Consider these developments:

• Twenty-eight million more women have joined the U.S. work force since 1950.

• Forty-six percent of the nation's women with children under six are employed.

• Sixty-three percent of the women with children aged six through seventeen are employed.

• In 1980, forty-eight percent of America's families in poverty were maintained by women.

• Numbers of women studying law, medicine, and business are increasing dramatically.

• Husband-wife households with one working spouse will account for only 14 percent of all U.S. households in 1990, compared with 43 percent in 1960.

"God could not be everywhere, and therefore he made mothers," reads a Hebrew proverb.

Caring motherhood is a blessing that today's world needs far more abundantly.

And as one Latter-day Saint husband of a childless companion once said to her, tenderly:

"You need not possess children to love them. Loving is not synonymous with possessing, and possessing is not necessarily loving. The world is filled with people to be loved, guided, taught, lifted, and inspired."[1]

Notes

1. Ardeth Greene Kapp, *All Kinds of Mothers* (Salt Lake City, Utah, Deseret Book Co., 1979), p. 11.

12

Touch of Heaven

This was Samoa, a group of fourteen tiny islands strewn like uncut emeralds in the vast Pacific, roughly a thousand miles south of the equator.

The day was Monday, February 16. The year: 1976.

It was a special day.

On the broad, fairway-like lawns of the Church College near Apia, some 150 Samoan men welcomed President Spencer W. Kimball with ceremonial dances generally reserved for only a visiting head of state.

They wore knee-length, black skirts, red and orange leis, and white bands around their black-haired heads, generally crewcut. Their light brown, pillar-like legs glistened as they cavorted like tribal warriors under a tropical sun.

After the pageantry, about a dozen Samoan men and women, in native garb, gathered in front of President Kimball, seated under a small bowery.

Together they began to sing:

"Our prophet dear, we need a temple here."

Through touching song, they told their leader they wanted to be united in the eternal marriage that comes only in the temple. They explained they could not afford the air fare to the nearest temple, in New Zealand, some two thousand miles away.

In 1976, there were sixteen temples in use—none in Asia, South America, Central America, or Africa. Only one temple was in use by the Church in the United States east of the Rocky Mountains—in metropolitan Washington, D.C.

Since 1976, ten new temples have been dedicated, in such far-flung places as São Paulo, Brazil; Tokyo, Japan; Seattle, Washington; Santiago, Chile; Mexico City; and in Tonga and in Tahiti.

On Friday, August 5, 1983 a sparkling white, single-spired temple, crowned with a heroic-size, gold-leafed Angel Moroni, was dedicated in Samoa. For some eighteen months before that dedication, hundreds of Samoan Saints, usually barefoot or wearing thongs, had toiled tirelessly on the construction of their own temple. Usually working with about thirty at a time, they had begun each work day joyously with a hymn and a prayer. Much of the work had been voluntary, without pay.

In May 1984 a new temple will be dedicated in Boise, Idaho. Ground will also be broken for a new temple in Denver, Colorado. Later in the year five more temples will be opened—in Sydney, Australia; Dallas, Texas; Taiwan; the Philippines; and Guatemala.

At the April 1984 general conference, President Gordon B. Hinckley reported that six additional temples will be dedicated in 1985; six more in 1986. Plans for five new temples were also announced.

Altogether since 1976, the Church leadership has announced thirty-one new temples. Some have been completed, some are under construction, and some are in the planning stage.

Included in that temple list are new edifices for all seven continents, except Antartica, plus five in islands of the Pacific, not counting the one dedicated in Japan in 1980.

Those thirty-one temples are almost twice the number (eighteen) of temples constructed by the Church in its first 144 years, up to 1976.

"Within the next few years it is probable that we shall have a temple within the reach of almost every Latter-day Saint in the world," President Hinckley said at a meeting of regional representatives and stake presidents prior to April general conference.

Temples are the only edifices where necessary and sacred ordinances can be performed for opening the way to "the greatest of all the gifts of God" (D&C 14:7): eternal life. For this, the ordinances must, of course, be coupled with righteous living.

Temples also provide the blessing of performing for the departed these same sacred ordinances, a service the deceased cannot perform for themselves.

Temples indeed are pathways to heavenly exaltation.

Temples also provide the golden cords that hold marriages and families together here and hereafter. Studies show that temple marriages are five times less likely to end in divorce than civil ones.

"I go to the temple once a month for spiritual renewal, to reaffirm my vows of fidelity," said a prominent LDS businessman and community leader. "That regular visit brings me a pause to reflect quietly on the basics of life, to help others unseen, to feast on a touch of heaven as in no other place."

Temples are indeed coming within reach of almost every Latter-day Saint. The key move now is for each of us to reach regularly for the temple, truly a "touch of heaven" on earth.

Pink Carnations

Omni was a warrior who lived in the ancient Americas at the same time Alexander the Great, astride his spirited black charger, was conquering much of the ancient world.

A book in the Book of Mormon is named for Omni. It is one of the volume's shortest books—only one chapter. Omni wrote only the first three verses.

Yet Omni wrote enough to give us a glimpse of himself. He said he fought "much with the sword to preserve my people, the Nephites."

He described himself as "a wicked man," explaining that "I have not kept the statutes and the commandments of the Lord as I ought to have done."

An engraven admission like that takes integrity.

Omni's last recorded verse gives us more about him to admire:

"And I had kept these plates according to the commandments of my fathers."

Then he adds that he conferred the plates upon his son Amaron. (See Omni 1:1–3.)

Omni honored his forebears in preserving their sacred records, adding to them, and in passing them on to a trusted son.

How a man or woman respects his forebears and those who have enriched his life is often a good measure of his character.

For many, if not most, members of the Church there comes a special day to pay tribute to those who have contributed much to our lives. It is Memorial Day.

In April 1984 a father with two of his daughters, one in her teens and the other older, visited Salt Lake's city cemetery. He guided them into the older sector of the large hillside burial park. They viewed graves of many of the stalwart leaders of the Church.

The three admired the marker over the remains of President Anthony W. Ivins, counselor to President Heber J. Grant. The marker was topped with a huge reddish petrified log, about thirty inches in diameter and thirty-six inches long. President Ivins loved the outdoors.

They observed the markers over graves of many other men and women who have made Church history.

"But what touched me most in that wonderful tour of the city cemetery," said the father, "was what I found between two small, flat headstones in the shade of two towering pines."

They were matching granite headstones, each approximately one by two feet. One was for Claude Q. Cannon, who died at forty-seven in 1930. The other: for Emily Cannon, who expired at fifty-nine in 1942.

Between the two headstones was a bouquet of sixteen fresh pink carnations attractively arranged amid leafy, dark green sprigs.

This was more than a month before Memorial Day. This was forty-two years after the death of one of the couple, fifty-four years after the other.

Yet someone still remembered, with fresh pink carnations!

Family ties today are strengthened as we turn our hearts to our fathers and mothers.

There are other benefits, too. Stringfellow Barr, an American educator, recalled the words of a veteran newspaperman:

"You know the trouble with the present generation? They've never read the minutes of the previous meeting."

One of the wise and respected leaders in his community is now eighty-seven years old—still clear and alert of mind. He has served as president of the chamber of commerce and local Rotary Club, and has been a giant in his profession, advertising.

His is a close-knit Latter-day Saint family, with children, grandchildren and great-grandchildren of achievement and goodness. A son is an Apostle.

Certainly a key to his nobility of character, of his grandeur as a sire is the way in which he[1] honors his companion.

She died almost a year ago, after they had been married nearly sixty-four years. For her last twelve years she was an invalid, victim of a stroke. Through all this time he waited on her tenderly, around the clock.

Now almost daily he visits her grave, always adorned with fresh flowers. He fastidiously grooms the lawn around her marker. In the winter he shoveled a path through the snow to her grave.

To friends who have thought he does all this mournfully, he has explained that this is not so. What he does is done cheerfully, lovingly.

Pink carnations. They can say so much so quietly.

Notes

1. Marion C. Nelson, father of Elder Russell M. Nelson of the Council of the Twelve.

14

Full Steam Ahead

Earlier this spring in a Mountain West city, a sixtyish Latter-day Saint couple were driving their four-door, silver-gray Mercedes to fast meeting for a grandchild's blessing.

The streets were wet. Sleet was falling.

As the couple's sedan slowed for a red light, a well-worn, low-slung car bolted out of a service station. There was a crash. No one was hurt. But there was a scar—a huge, deep dent in the rear door on the driver's side of the Mercedes.

Two youths, appearing to be in their late teens, jumped out of the worn car.

"Our windshield was steamed," apologetically said the shorter youth, the front-seat passenger.

"Sorry," said the taller slender youth, the driver. "I was at fault." He readily gave his name, his father's name, address, and phone number—and volunteered his car insurance policy number.

The older man expressed dismay at the youth's careless driving. But he spoke appreciation for the young driver's forthrightness, integrity.

Some 2,380,000 teens across the United States, and more in Canada and other countries, are graduating from high school this late spring. Perhaps that young car driver is typical of many, if not most, of these graduates:

Eager to move "full steam ahead."

Feasting on the joy of the morning of life.

"Green in judgment," and wearing the "rose of youth," in the words of Shakespeare.

Honest.

Facing perhaps more exciting choices for a life's work than have ever been spread before high school graduates—in a wondrously unfolding Information Age.

Also, never before have there been so many beckoning elements for "steaming up" a young person's vision.

"Many reach legal adulthood at age eighteen ill-prepared for today's environment, which is so battered with the constant drumbeat of sex, crime and violence," wrote Richard G. Capen, Jr., publisher of the *Miami Herald*. "It's everywhere: in their neighborhoods, on television and in movies, and in popular songs."

However, Mr. Capen notes, encouragingly, "some positive trends." He reports that University of Miami's fastest-growing department is its religion department, where enrollment has tripled in five years. He adds that more than forty University of Miami football players, who completed the 1983-84 season as the nation's No. 1 rated college team, each week participate in Bible study, pregame services, and meditation.

He cites a Gallup poll showing the number of people between eighteen and twenty-nine years of age participating in religious education has more than doubled in four years, to 35 percent.

Attendance of Latter-day Saint youth in seminary is encouraging, too.

At high schools where release-time seminary is available, 82 percent of Latter-day Saint students in 1982 were enrolled, up from 72 percent five years before. Where early-morning seminary prevails, the percentage climbed from 61 in 1978 to 64 in 1982.

But these are statistics. Heartwarming are the cases where "steam is being cleared from windshields" through seminary:

In one Midwestern high school, an LDS youth found his way into seminary. His father was inactive in the Church, an alcoholic. In his high school senior year, he had become alcoholic, too.

One morning the seminary lesson was on Solomon, when he was given the opportunity to ask whatever he wanted from the Lord. The teacher asked each class member to write on a piece of paper what he or she would want from the Lord if given Solomon's opportunity.

The alcoholic youth wrote:

"I would just wish I could be a better person because I'm not any good to anyone."

The caring teacher was touched. Periodically she visited the youth, encouraging him. This spring, he told his seminary teacher he had voluntarily enrolled in an alcoholic treatment program. He continues to progress, with his seminary teacher helping all along.

In Georgia five Latter-day Saint high school girls were celebrating the birthday anniversary of one of them with an overnight slumber party. On the spur of the moment, they decided to attend a movie. Part way through the movie, one of the girls excused herself, and phoned her father to pick her up, saying she was not feeling well. When he arrived at the theater, he found his daughter outside, in tears.

On the drive home, she explained that the movie had become distastefully sexy.

Her father suggested next day at school she tell the other four girls why she had left the theater. She did. They all commended her. They said they felt the same way, but did not leave the theater because they did not want to offend the others. Then they said to the girl who had left: "We look to you for our example."

Asked where she received her strength, she replied that her source was in attending seminary regularly and reading the scriptures.

Most recent estimates (in 1980) show approximately 85 percent of young men completing seminary fulfill missions.

Similarly, a high percentage of graduates are married in the temple.

Graduation is a happy time.

It is a time, too, to move into adulthood full steam ahead— without "steam on the windshield."

And seminary really helps!

15

Listen When You Pray

He was adviser to kings. He was both poet and prophet, a family man. He began to prophesy in Jerusalem about 740 B.C., the time of the founding of Rome, some one thousand miles away.

This "prince of prophets" was quoted more than any other Old Testament author by Jesus, whose earthly mission he foretold, lofty after lofty verse.

He was Isaiah, son of Amoz. More chapters in the Bible bear Isaiah's name than any other.

Declared the Lord, as recorded in Isaiah: "Incline your ear, and come unto me: hear, and your soul shall live." (Isaiah 55:3.)

Most of us pray. How often do we listen when we pray, as the Lord seems to suggest in Isaiah?

Luke tells us that the evening before Jesus chose His Twelve Apostles, He departed to a mountain, "and continued all night in prayer to God." (Luke 6:12.)

Surely the Master was not talking continuously in prayer through the night. He must have listened—much.

Again, after feeding the five thousand with the miracle of the loaves and fishes, Jesus secluded Himself on a mountain "to pray." Matthew records He was there for the night. Again, He must have inclined His ear to His Father as He supplicated.

To listen when we pray is to expect, to await response, silent as it may be.

"Thy servant heareth," said the boy Samuel to the Lord some three hundred years before Isaiah's day. (1 Samuel 3:10.) And Samuel became a mighty prophet, the founder of Israel's kingdom.

With that fourteen-year-old farm boy's first spoken prayer in wooded western New York state in 1820, came the Father's command to "hear." Said the Father to Joseph Smith: *This is My Beloved Son. Hear Him!*" (JS—H 1:17.)

And because Joseph Smith *listened* then and for years afterward, the great Restoration unfolded.

Helen Keller, the Alabama dynamo whose sight and hearing left her before she was two and who became an international lecturer and author, wrote much about faith and prayer. She also spoke of hearing, though deaf, the Lord's response: "The word of God came unto me, sitting alone among the multitude."[1]

Because we do not listen when we pray, is it not true that often:

—Our blessing of the food becomes a signal to eat rather than a benediction and a thanks.

—Our bedside prayer, more a recitation than a supplication.

—Our unscheduled prayer, an SOS instead of a sublime pause and request for strength, assurance, and peace.

As we use computers more, there is the temptation to "computerize" prayer.

When we pray, how ennobling it could be to listen with the spirit of Job of Uz. He lost his ten children, his thousands upon thousands of sheep, camels, oxen, and asses, and was stricken with boils—yet thanked and praised God.

"Stand still, and consider the wondrous works of God." (Job 37:14.)

Notes

1. *The Faith of Helen Keller*, Kansas City, Mo., Hallmark Editions, 1967, page 34.

16

Noblest of Names

The title of "father of his country" was bestowed on Marcus Tullius Cicero, the great Roman defense lawyer, orator, author, and government leader.

That was some sixty years before the birth of Christ.

The Russian Senate in 1721 gave Peter the Great the same title. George Washington to this day is called "father of his country" in the United States.

Hippocrates, the eminent Greek physician and surgeon who lived four centuries before Jesus, now continues to be called the "father of medicine."

Alfred the Great has been esteemed as "father of English prose," and Izaak Walton, as "father of angling."

But perhaps the greatest compliment on fatherhood came from God Himself to a wealthy cattleman, astronomer, warrior, and prophet.

Of him, Abraham son of Terah, Jehovah said:

"For I know him, that he will command his children and his household after him, and they shall keep the way of the Lord, to do justice and judgment." (Genesis 18:19.)

Shortly before, the Lord changed the great prophet's name from Abram, meaning "exalted father" to Abraham, meaning "father of a multitude." Abraham also became "father of faithful" and father of God's covenant people.

The Lord's tribute to Abraham some four thousand years ago is timely counsel today.

Father Abraham was concerned about Sodom and Gomorrah. Many noble fathers today are similarly worried about the growing mass of sex, smut, and violence beckoning their youth on television, in motion pictures, and the printed page.

As many peoples observe Father's Day, it is a time to pay tribute to fathers—and for fathers to ponder their sacred role as leaders in the basic unit of the Church and society: the home.

George Herbert, the seventeenth-century violin-playing British author, wrote: "One father is more than a hundred schoolmasters."

There is a leading banker[1] in America's West who probably serves on more major corporate boards than any other in his state. Yet he is sill in his forty's. But many of his friends will tell you his most noteworthy achievement is as a father.

If one of his three daughters is in a school play, marching with the pep club, or competing in a tennis tournament, he will likely be there. He will travel all night or miss a board meeting to cheer his son at a ski meet. He loves cooking popcorn in a pan for the family. Often you see him with all his family, dressed in their Sunday best, at civic functions.

Another devoted father[2] with nine children operates a small insurance agency out of his home. He earns extra income as a carpenter, barbers his children's hair. He has an agreement with his sons: he funds half their missions; they earn the other half, as newsboys or with other jobs. The two eldest sons have completed missions, one is serving now. The other four are saving for missions. Two children have graduated from college. Two are currently enrolled.

The seven daughters of Bryant S. Hinckley (1867-1971), Lincolnesque teacher who was a stake president eleven years, compiled some of his messages in a book. One tells of a teacher in a school district near Indianapolis asking 326 children to write what each thought of his or her father.

The comments were to be unsigned. Replies were to be read at a PTA meeting.

The announcement drew a big attendance. Parents came in small cars and big ones. There were a bank president, utility magnate, laborer, baker, tailor, and others.

At the meeting the PTA president read replies at random. Many began "I like my daddy." Some of the reasons: he built my doll house, takes me to the park, taught me to shoot.

"Not one child mentioned his family house, car, neighborhood, food, or clothing."

President David O. McKay said: "No other success can compensate for failure in the home."

It was this same President McKay, who when a member of the First Presidency in 1935, drove some three hundred miles round trip to witness a high school play his twentyish daughter, Emma Rae, directed in a little Idaho farm town, McCammon.

William Wordsworth, the English poet, lost his mother at eight, his father at thirteen. Wordsworth, Queen Victoria's poet laureate, wrote a truth grandly: "Father! to God himself we cannot give a holier name."

Notes

1. Spencer Fox Eccles.

2. Farrell D. Jensen, member, Salt Lake Granite Park Stake presidency.

17

Friend Inside

Few men influenced America in the mid-1800s like Abraham Lincoln and Brigham Young.

Few who lived in that period continue to influence the world today as do they.

Lincoln proved to the world that democracy works, that it can endure the test of a bitter division in a nation that erupted into a terrible war. Few men in history have spoken with such eloquence, few have lived so nobly in high public office.

Brigham Young led one of the great exoduses of all time. He was leader in the founding of several hundred cities and towns in an uninviting mountain wilderness. As a spiritual giant, he directed a global effort in teaching the restored gospel of Jesus Christ—against great odds.

Brigham Young was born eight years before Abraham Lincoln and lived twelve years after the emancipator's assassination.

Both were self-made. Brigham Young had eleven days of formal schooling; Lincoln less than a year. Brigham's mother died when he was thirteen; Abraham's, when he was nine.

Brigham began his own business at sixteen. He was a carpenter, painter, and glazier. Abraham began hiring out as a youth. He was a rail splitter, farm hand. Until he was twenty-two he remained with his farmer father.

Both were deeply religious, Bible readers beginning early in life. Both admired George Washington.

Lincoln reached six feet, four inches in height, was angular, dark-skinned and strong. His coarse black hair "stood on end."

Brigham Young was medium height, broad-shouldered, sandy-haired, blue-eyed.

In 1846 when Brigham and the Mormons began the exodus from Nauvoo in west central Illinois, Lincoln in Illinois was first elected to the U.S. House of Representatives.

Both demonstrated powerfully in their lives self-reliance and service to others—the theme of stake conferences during the second half of 1984.

The year before his tragic death in 1865, President Lincoln replied to a Missouri committee:

"I desire so to conduct the affairs of this administration that if at the end, when I come to lay down the reins of power, I have lost every other friend on earth, I shall at least have one friend left, and that friend shall be down inside of me."

Four years later, in the recently completed Salt Lake Tabernacle, built under his direction, President Young declared at general conference:[1]

"Brethren, learn. You have learned a good deal, it is true; but learn more; learn to sustain yourselves; lay up grain and flour, and save it against a day of scarcity. Sisters, do not ask your husbands to sell the last bushel of grain you have to buy something for you out of the stores, but aid your husbands in storing it up against a day of want, and always have a year's, or two, provision on hand."

The joy of service to others begins with self-respect, as described by President Lincoln, with self-preparedness, as told by President Young.

Around the world today, Church members continue to show organized helpfulness.

In the Twentieth Ward, Mesa Arizona Maricopa Stake, high

priests earlier this year reroofed the home of a man stricken with emphysema. Later, in the same ward, members reroofed a struggling widow's home. In the same stake, three years ago, Boy Scouts reroofed the meetinghouse of the Church of God in Christ.

For some eight months last year, each evening for thirty to forty-five minutes, a different member assigned by the high priests provided physical therapy to a brother who had suffered a stroke—in Bellevue Seventh Ward, Bellevue Washington Stake.

Young priests in Norcross Ward, Sandy Springs Georgia Stake, this year dug a plumbing line to the home of a ward member stricken with paralysis. They also took the sacrament to his home each Sabbath.

In this same Georgia ward, a well-educated, elderly sister developed a brain disorder. The ward Young Women wash her windows, scrub her floors, and do other household chores. Young Men do her yard work. Relief Society members help with meals, get groceries. The visiting teachers bring her medication.

That friend "inside of me," described by Lincoln, glows warmly through service to others. A helping hand brings heaven closer, too. Benjamin, the prophet-king, speaking from a tower near the temple to a multitude amid tents, declared: "When ye are in the service of your fellow beings ye are only in the service of your God." (Mosiah 2:17.)

Notes

1. April 8, 1868.

18

Election Years:
1844 and 1984

The year 1844 was a presidential election year in the United States. There were only twenty-six states in the Union.

The first "dark horse" presidential candidate emerged that year. He was James K. Polk, a bright little attorney, a hard worker, who five years before had been elected governor of Tennessee. He had lost in two subsequent bids for the governorship.

There was a deadlock in 1844 in the Democratic convention between the two leading presidential candidates: Martin Van Buren, a former president, and Lewis Cass of Michigan, a former U.S. minister to France. Polk became the compromise candidate. His opponent was Henry Clay, the well-known Whig from Kentucky. A Whig slogan was "Who is James K. Polk?" Polk's slogan was "54—40 or Fight!" This meant the U.S. should have all the Oregon territory, north to the latitude of 50 degrees 40 minutes, even if it meant war with Britain.

Polk won that year.

On June 27 that same year an event occurred in a little Illinois prairie town of some four hundred people that caused far less attention than the presidential campaign. Joseph Smith, the 38-year-old prophet leader of the Mormons, was martyred that day by a mob with painted faces in the two-story stone jail in Carthage, seat of Hancock County, Illinois.

Joseph Smith was much less known at his death in 1844 than James K. Polk, when he died, white-haired at fifty-three, five years later.

When the prophet was martyred there were only 26,146 members of the Church. They were a driven people.

In this presidential year of 1984, how does the Prophet Joseph Smith measure in achievement?

• The Church he founded 154 years ago is approaching six million members. *U.S. News and World Report*[1] notes that the Church in the United States during the decade beginning 1973 showed a 40 percent increase in membership, while most mainline Protestant churches were losing membership.

• There are now more than 13,994 wards and branches (congregations) of the Church worldwide, all directed by an unpaid ministry.

• In 1984 there are more than twenty-seven thousand full-time Church missionaries, most of them young men and women, serving in 90 countries at their own expense or that of their parents.

• While the membership of the church during the past fifty years has increased 7.4 times, attendance at sacrament meetings has increased much more dramatically. With far more members, the percentage of total members attending has more than doubled.

• In 1830 Joseph Smith presented to the world the first printed edition of the Book of Mormon with five thousand copies. Today, the Book has been printed in thirty-nine different languages. Approximately a million copies are now printed each year.

• In 1833, at age twenty-seven, Joseph Smith issued a revelation known as the Word of Wisdom, proscribing the use of tobacco and alcohol as injurious to health. In 1984 the United States Surgeon General predicted, with use of tobacco in the nation declining dramatically, that by the year 2000 the U.S. could be a "smokeless society."

• In Utah, where the population today is 70 percent Latter-day Saint:

—Incidence of cancer is 25 percent below the national average and is lowest among the 50 states.

—Utah ranks first among the 50 states in the median number of school years completed by the adult population (eighteen years and older): 12.8 (Utah); 12.5 (U.S.A.).

—Utah is first in the percentage of adults with high school diplomas: 80.2 percent (Utah); 66.6 percent (U.S.A.).

—In a nationwide survey conducted among the 18,000 members of the Association of Master of Business Administration (MBA) executives in 1977, Salt Lake City rated first among America's major cities as the best place in which to live. Reasons for the top rating: safety, cleanliness, natural beauty.

• During the past thirty years, four times America's Mother of the Year has been a Latter-day Saint.

• In 1983, the percentage of available United States Latter-day Saint youth enrolled in Boy Scouts was 82, compared to the nation's less than 20.

• Because of Joseph Smith's teaching of vicarious temple work for the dead, the Church today has in Salt Lake City the world's largest depository of genealogical records.

• In April, 1984 the Church had 896 chapels under construction worldwide.

• The Salt Lake Mormon Tabernacle Choir today provides the oldest continuous network radio program (since 1929) in the history of radio.

• The Church owns and operates the largest private university in enrollment in America: Brigham Young University.

Measuring Joseph Smith between the two presidential election years of 1844 and 1984 presents him as a man of tremendous achievement. His stature will continue to grow with the years, decades, and centuries because he was indeed a prophet of God, the mighty restoring instrument of the Church of Jesus Christ in the latter days.

Brigham Young said:

"I feel like shouting hallelujah, all the time, when I think that I ever knew Joseph Smith."

Notes

1. April 30, 1984.

19

All-American

Thomas Jefferson was born in a plain frame home on a slight rise in a forest clearing four miles from the village of Charlottesville, Virginia. It was April 13, 1743.

Jefferson was the third child and eldest son of ten children.

Young Tom, red-haired, angular, freckled, and with blue-gray eyes, adored his farmer father, Peter Jefferson. His father was tough, hard and long-working, sound in judgment, liberty-loving, well-read but unschooled—and strong as a bull.

In his father's small library young Tom feasted on the Bible, Shakespeare, Addison, Swift, and Steele.

Rugged, honest Peter Jefferson was a leader among the neighboring farmers. He was a man of the people. He often hosted nearby Indians in his home.

When Tom was thirteen, his father died.

At sixteen, Jefferson on his own entered Virginia's august William and Mary College.

Here in Williamsburg, Virginia, Tom Jefferson continued to show he loved liberty. But he also demonstrated how man can flower into balanced and brilliant greatness when that liberty is matched with a love of learning and culture, of family and people —and a self-discipline that was awesome.

Williamsburg, when tall, arrow-straight Jefferson came into town, was the colonial capital with some two hundred homes, mostly frame.

During sessions of the legislature, Williamsburg expanded in size and social life. Rich planters brought to the capital their wives and daughters, fluttering with feathers, silk, ribbons, and lace, and riding in coaches drawn by six horses. Gentlemen wore velvet and buckles.

Tom Jefferson, the wealthy student, mingled in all this—the elegant minuets, quadrilles, and Virginia reels. He attended the theater, admired the race horses, and was popular with the young ladies.

Though still a youth, he also became a close friend of three unusual minds:

William Small, Scottish professor of mathematics, deep thinker, and philosopher.

Judge George Wythe, "foremost jurist in colonial Virginia," whom Jefferson described as his second father.

Virginia's royal governor, Francis Fauquier, a refined intellectual with broad interests and acquaintances.

Together the four dined and talked—about politics, poetry, and other subjects. Each week there was a drawing room concert with Jefferson playing the violin.

In his second year at William and Mary, Jefferson gave up much of his social life, his horse, his fox hunting—and bore down on his studies fifteen hours a day. For exercise he daily ran a mile out of town and back.

Jefferson then studied and practiced law in Williamsburg, with distinction. He also continued to look after his large farm, always testing and experimenting with crops. Near his birthplace he designed and built for his family his red brick, thirty-five-room home, Monticello. He filled it with his ingenious inventions, from a dumbwaiter to a revolving chair.

In June 1776 the American colonies' Continental Congress named a committee to draft a declaration of independence. The committee: Jefferson, John Adams, Benjamin Franklin, Roger

Sherman, and Robert Livingston. The committee unanimously asked Jefferson, only thirty-three, to prepare the draft. Few changes were made.

The Declaration was adopted by Congress on July 4, 1776.

Several months later, Jefferson resigned from Congress and returned to Virginia's House of Delegates. Jefferson's bills there separated the Anglican Church from the state. No longer were its clergymen paid with taxes. Ten years later, when Jefferson was minister to France, Virginia's assembly passed his Statue of Religious Freedom, assuring religious freedom in Virginia.

Jefferson was still in France in 1787 when the Constitution of the United States was framed. Jefferson's close friend, scholarly, wispy James Madison, who has been called the "Father of the Constitution," sent Jefferson a draft. Jefferson approved it, but urged a bill of rights. Madison then introduced the ten amendments that became the Bill of Rights.

Jefferson played a key role in bringing religious freedom to America, in preparing the way for the restoration of the Church of Jesus Christ—occurring just four years after Jefferson's death at eighty-three on July 4, 1826—the fiftieth anniversary of the adoption of his Declaration of Independence.

Thomas Jefferson served as governor of Virginia, Washington's secretary of state, United States president, and founding president of University of Virginia. His library became the nucleus of the Library of Congress. Perhaps no one ever served as president of the United States whose brain sponged up so much and contributed so much in so many disciplines.

One of Jefferson's biographers, Claude G. Bowers, distinguished New York editorial writer and diplomat, wrote in the preface:

"But no one can read this story without marveling at the Providence that guided us to independence and nationhood and to dignity and stability as a nation."[1]

Jefferson, in his later years, wrote:

"To love God with all thy heart and thy neighbor as thyself is the sum of religion."

Thomas Jefferson gave so much to bring under government the free agency to which all men and women as children of God are entitled. He also demonstrated magnificently how to use that freedom in a disciplined quest for the glory of intelligence, then sharing it broadly.

To all America, and all the world, Thomas Jefferson was truly an all-American.

Notes

1. Bowers, Claude G., *The Young Jefferson*, (Boston, Mass., Houghton Mifflin Company, 1945), p. vi.

20

A Somebody Sacred

It was the late afternoon rush hour on a busy thoroughfare in a western city.

Standing all alone in the second lane was a blond tot clad only in a diaper. Cars roared by.

A woman newspaper reporter, making a left hand turn, braked her light green sedan. She jumped out, leaving her car blocking traffic. She swooped the child into her arms, carried him to the curb. There she inquired of a teenage boy and others where the tot lived. After several door stops she found his home, in a little apartment behind business offices.

The reporter knocked hard and long then shouted: "I have your child out here. I found him in the street."

The door opened. A woman, apparently the tot's mother, continued talking on the phone as she responded at the door. The reporter told the woman where she had found the child, that he could have been killed. Still with phone in hand, the woman accepted the child, but gave no answer.

The reporter returned to her car, still blocking traffic. As she drove away, she debated whether to phone police or other authorities. She wondered what she could say. She did not call.

In a nearby city, a slender, quiet pharmacist recently was speaking at a funeral. It was for his own daughter, a little girl not yet four years old. At twenty-three months the child had contracted a disease that inflamed her muscles. For days that stretched into weeks and months and almost two years the little girl had been in constant pain all over her body. Through the long, agonizing nights, as well as days, her parents had caressed her tenderly. Together and singly they had been at her side in Primary Children's Medical Center.

At the funeral, the father spoke gratefully of the privilege of parenting that child of pain. He spoke of her courage and tenacity, of her "pleases" and "thank yous" to nurses and doctors in the hospital, of her deciding with him which football team on TV they would support. He recalled lovingly her final night "when she got so silly with a gallon of milk and a bottle cap."

He likened her suffering to that of her Savior and of the prophet Abinadi. He expressed thanks for "the opportunity to care for one of the choicest spirits to ever grace the earth."

Two incidents. Two tots. Two parents.

With one there was neglect, child abuse.

With the other, child esteem.

There is probably much of both in your neighborhood and ours.

Unfortunately, child abuse—severe neglect, cruel physical hurt, sordid sexual abuse—is growing, alarmingly. Sadly, most of this activity is hidden, within the walls of homes.

Last year approximately a million cases of child abuse were reported in the United States. Far more cases go unreported, authorities say. Sexual abuse, it is estimated, now occurs in one of every eight to ten homes.

Latter-day Saint homes, sorrowfully, are not immune.

But much can be done to help, and many there are who are willing.

"The vast majority of child abusers are not bad people," affirms husky, fiftyish Dr. William Martin (Marty) Palmer, pediatrician at the Primary Children's Medical Center and the University of Utah Medical Center. Each year he treats or examines hundreds of victims of child abuse.

"Child abusers are generally people under stress, many of

them parents who have moved to a new city without friends or relatives. They may be under stress for financial or marital reasons."

Visiting teachers and home teachers can help. Neighbors can warmly welcome new move-ins, let them know there is someone nearby who cares.

Latter-day Saints can demonstrate the joy of selfless, loving parenthood. For example, one couple now in their sixty's have cared affectionately for over twenty-five years for a retarded son who has never been able to walk or talk.

In our homes we must continually teach and act this truth:

Each tot is divine, a literal child of God.

Jesus, rebuking those who protested the bringing of little ones to Him, said:

"Suffer the little children to come unto me . . . for of such is the kingdom of God." (Mark 10:14.)

That tot whining through the night, breaking a precious dish, or walking mud across the livingroom carpet is still a child of God.

He or she needs discipline at times, with love.

Always that tot deserves respect, as a *somebody* sacred!

21

Fit for the Olympics

It will be a day to remember: Saturday, July 28, 1984.

There will be a flourish of heraldic trumpets. A fluttering cloud of four thousand white homing pigeons will be released over some 100,000 spectators in the Coliseum in Los Angeles. Thousands of colorfully uniformed athletes from over 130 countries will parade onto the well-groomed green turf.

A runner, bearing a torch originating in Greece and carried by relay through ten thousand legs in the United States, will climb stairs and light a flame. It will burn throughout the XXIII Olympiad.

A former sportscaster, President Ronald Wilson Reagan, will proclaim:

"I declare open the Olympic Games of Los Angeles, celebrating the Twenty-third Olympiad of the modern era."

For the next fifteen days, champion athletes of the free world will compete in track and field, canoeing, basketball, swimming, and many other events. At least eight Latter-day Saints[1] will be among them.

Olympic records continue to improve with the years. For example:

A twenty-two-year-old Harvard University student, Ellery Clark, won the high jump at the first modern Olympiad in Greece in 1896 with a leap of 5 feet 11¼ inches. Alma Richards, a tall, awkward-looking Mormon from Parowan, Utah, won the event in Stockholm in 1912, soaring 6 feet 4 inches for an Olympic record. In Moscow, Gerd Wessig, a 6-foot 5-inch cook from the German Democratic Republic, jumped 7 feet 8¾ inches for an Olympic and world record in 1980—almost two feet higher than the 1896 record!

The Olympic record for the 100-meter dash has been reduced over 2 full seconds from the 12-second time in 1896. The 1,500-meter run time has been trimmed from 4 minutes 33.2 seconds to 3 minutes 34.9 seconds.

Perhaps never since the modern Olympics began eighty-eight years ago has there been so much world attention given physical fitness as now.

It is reported that more than two thousand U.S. hotels today offer fitness facilities—a tenfold increase in three years.

The U.S. Surgeon General, Dr. C. Everett Koop, this spring reported a 7 percent decline in the nation's cigarette smoking in 1983. He said America's No. 1 health goal should be "a smoke-free society by the year 2000."

President Reagan at seventy-three is the oldest U.S. President in history. Yet as he seeks reelection, age is not a significant campaign issue. At six-foot one-inch and 194 pounds, he keeps fit with the treadmill, exercycle, and gymnastics—and does much wood chopping at his California ranch. He watches calories, and his diet includes "lots of salads and vegetables."

Of the seven men who were originally Democratic candidates for president, plus President Reagan and Vice President Bush, none smokes cigarettes.

The *Wall Street Journal*[2] reports:

"Signs of sobriety abound. . . . Per capita use of distilled spirits has declined every year since 1980.

" 'If you are at a party now and say you don't want a drink, no one looks at you like you're crazy,' says Kris Hefley, research director of Denver-based Westrend Group, a firm that consults with corporations on social change."

This summer, aiming to reduce highway deaths, Congress passed legislation that in effect lifts the drinking age nationwide to twenty-one.

As hundreds of millions of television viewers in more than a hundred countries cheer their olympiad favorites, Latter-day Saints can gratefully cheer this fact:

More than a hundred years ago, the Lord gave to the Prophet Joseph Smith a revelation known as the Word of Wisdom. It proscribes the use of strong drinks, tobacco, and hot drinks. It encourages the eating of herbs, fruits, and grains.

This is a pattern to which a fitness-minded world today is more and more turning.

Notes

1. Henry Marsh, 3,000-meter steeplechase; Paul Cummings, 10,000-meter run; Doug Padilla, 5,000-meter run; Peter Vidmar, gymnastics; Lorna Griffin, women's shot put and discus; and Walt Zobell, international trap shooting—all representing the United States; Stefan Fernholm discus, Sweden; and Karl Tilleman, basketball, Canada.

2. March 14, 1984.

22

A Mighty Symbol

"Looming with solemn authority, the granite bastion of the Mormon Temple lifts six graceful spires, the tallest crowned by a golden angel."

Thus is the Salt Lake Temple described by a new book published by the National Geographic Society: *Exploring America's Valleys.*

The *National Geographic* magazine itself, in an eighteen-page article on Utah and the Mormons, in 1975 termed it "the great temple."

The London *Times* a year later said it was "a striking and unusual building."

Russell Chandler in the Los Angeles *Times* in 1983 wrote of "the magnificent Temple Square" and "the Latter-day Saints' holiest shrine, the lofty, chiseled granite Salt Lake Temple."

An impressive new book is titled *The Salt Lake Temple, a Monument to Its People.*

The holy edifice is indeed one of America's landmarks, the shining symbol of the Church to the world.

Temple Square continues to be a tourist attraction, with 2.4 million visitors in 1983, approximately the same as visited Yellowstone Park.

Consider now the beginnings of that widely acclaimed structure:

Four days after his arrival in desolate, sage-shawled Salt Lake Valley on July 24, 1847, President Brigham Young designated the site for building a temple. It was in an isolated wilderness some thousand miles from the main body of the Saints on the Missouri River.

Less than six years later, on that spot, ground was broken to begin construction of the temple. It was Monday, February 14, 1853. The sky was clear. One to three inches of snow covered the ground. There were six inches of frost in the earth. Great Salt Lake City's population was 6,157.

Most of the inhabitants lived in log or adobe cabins. Many of these settlers had been driven from comfortable brick homes in Nauvoo.

At the ground breaking, Brigham Young spoke to the assembled several thousands from a buggy. (He once said that "not one of four of my family had shoes to their feet when we came to this valley.")

A band played "Auld Lang Syne." There was a prayer of consecration by President Heber C. Kimball of the First Presidency.

Some of the men in the throng came with their tools, and "much earth was removed that afternoon."

Truman O. Angell, the temple architect, was there supervising the survey of the site.

For years he was to toil with his drawing pencil in a dim shack on the Temple Block, scaling and numbering each stone. His eyes sored. Insomnia plagued him. When his two-year-old son died, he drove the coffin to the cemetery in a borrowed wagon. He helped the grave digger cover the little box. Next day he was back on the job on the Temple Block.

But to return to 1853, the year temple construction started:

The pioneers were struggling to tame unruly and thirsty Salt Lake Valley. But they looked beyond. Brigham Young called stalwart men and women to establish new settlements in the rugged Rockies and desolate deserts. Mormon colonizers founded more than three hundred communities in the Mountain West.

But these high-booted men and sunbonneted women also reached spiritually to the outside—globally.

The year before the temple ground breaking, from Salt Lake

Valley more than a hundred missionaries were called to take the restored gospel of Jesus Christ to distant climes. Men like Kentucky-born Hosea Stout left for China. Canute Peterson, still in his twenties, was called to his native Norway. Others left for Siam, South Africa, Germany, India, the West Indies, and elsewhere.

In 1853, when the ground breaking occurred, new missions were opened in Malta, Africa, and Gibraltar.

As we honor our Mormon pioneers this week on the anniversary of their entrance into Salt Lake Valley, we admire them for their faith-fueled courage.

We can also esteem them because they thought and acted big.

While they struggled with a new kind of farming, with irrigation, in the desert, they started building a splendrous temple that would win the admiration of the world.

Why?

They were building the kingdom of God on earth, and they knew it.

They lived like kingdom builders.

Truman O. Angell, that humble, hard-toiling, gifted architect, wrote in his journal:

"I do feel well in doing all my ability will permit me to do if it end (sic) in the building of the Kingdom of God."

He described his work as a "calling" rather than a position or a job.

Today the kingdom continues abuilding. Happy is the man or woman who ever realizes he or she is part of the process.

And who thinks and acts big, as did our noble pioneers.

23

Competitor
with Love

He was a peasant, probably a shepherd, from the little Greek village of Maroussi, twenty miles northeast of Athens. He was twenty-four.

His name was Spiridon Louis (or Loues). With sixteen other entrants, he stood on the Marathon Bridge—26 miles, 385 yards from the big stadium in Athens.

This was the start of the marathon, the premier event in the first modern Olympiad, in 1896.

The Olympics had been held in ancient Greece every four years without interruption for at least 1,170 years. They had begun in 776 B.C., about the time Isaiah started to prophesy. The ancient Games were discontinued in A.D. 394.

A month before the 1896 Games, in Greece's Olympic trials, Louis had finished fifth among thirty-eight runners in the Marathon. (The event was named for the run of a valiant Greek messenger bringing the news to Athens of his country's victory over the invading Persians in 490 B.C. at Marathon.)

Now, in 1896, excitement was high in Greece.

There were four foreign aces among the seventeen who began the Olympic marathon on that April day.

Some hundred thousand spectators awaited the finish in the huge Athens Stadium. Among them were the king of Greece, the king of Serbia, government and business leaders, and the diplomatic corps.

As the race began, the French runner, Albin Lermusiaux, took an early lead. He was far ahead at the halfway mark. In the village of Karavati, a triumphal arch had been built. The villagers crowned the French runner with a floral wreath as he continued the grueling pace. He faltered, and a London-based Australian accountant, Edwin Flack, moved ahead. Four kilometers from the stadium, a delirious Flack gave up.

A Greek major astride a horse rushed through the stadium's marble entrance to the royal box. His report: a Greek was ahead, coming into the stadium.

Across the vast crowd were shouts, *"Elleen! Elleen!"* ("A Greek! A Greek!")

The little peasant, dusty and sweaty, entered the stadium. There was a thunderous roar. Two royal princes ran beside Louis in the stadium to the finish line.

Not only Greece, but also the world that day cheered Spiridon Louis, who, it was reported, had spent the previous night fasting and praying.

Officials, admiring women, and merchants showered Louis with jewelry, watches, offers for free clothing for life, monthly stipends, and other rich gifts. He turned them all down, it was reported, except a horse and a cart to help haul water to his village.

Spiridon Louis was rediscovered in 1936 when the Olympic Games were held in Adolf Hitler's Berlin. There the humble Greek peasant presented the militant dictator a laurel wreath from a hallowed grove at Olympia.

Louis died March 27, 1940.

"More than any single event, the victory of Spiridon Louis served as an inspiration to keep the Olympics going through the hard times that the movement faced over the next twelve years," wrote David Wallechinsky in his brilliantly authored *The Complete Book of the Olympics.*[1]

Spiridon Louis was a fierce competitor with gentle love for his fellow men.

The Olympics have been impressive gatherings of champions of various races from many walks of life—blacks from Africa and the United States; Orientals from China, Japan, and Korea; and Latins, Caucasians, and others—and one of the greatest champions of them all, an American Indian and orphan at fifteen, Jim Thorpe, hero of the 1912 Olympiad in Stockholm.

The Games remind us of an enduring truth spoken by a mighty prophet, Nephi, who died in the Western Hemisphere about the time of the Battle of Marathon in Greece: "He [the Lord] inviteth them all to come unto him and partake of his goodness . . . black and white, bond and free, male and female . . . all are alike unto God." (2 Nephi 26:33.)

This is a competitive world, as indeed it should be.

But, as the 1984 Olympics continue, it is well to remember: in the courts and legislative halls, in the professions, and on the playgrounds and playing fields, it is praiseworthy to battle fairly and hard. It is nobler to also extend helpful love to all mankind regardless of race and station—as children of God, all alike before Him.

That seemed to be the message of Spiridon Louis, the first hero of the modern Olympics.

Notes

1. New York, The Viking Press and Penguin Books, 1984.

24

Your Priceless Privilege

Pretty Jane Crezee (pronounced Crehzay) has blue eyes and light brown hair and is eighteen. Her ancestry is Dutch on both sides. Her home is in Sonora, a little lumbering town in the Sierra Mountains, some 125 miles east of San Francisco. Jane's father is a retired government geologist.

Jane was a homecoming queen finalist and cheerleader of Sonora High. She is the youngest of six children, all of whom have attended BYU. This fall she begins her sophomore year at BYU, majoring in dance and sign language. ("I plan to teach dance and gymnastics to the deaf.")

For the first time, this fall, Jane will do something entirely different—vote as a United States citizen.

"I'm preparing now to vote as an absentee," says Jane, "because I'll be at BYU in November. You may be sure I will vote, and I'm going to study the candidates and issues."

Jane is one of some 7.8 million Americans eighteen or nineteen years old who will be eligible to vote in a general election for the first time this year.

All told, the U.S. voting-age population this year is approximately 175 million. If the pattern in the previous presidential election (1980) follows, only 53.9 percent of them will cast a ballot.

The percentage should be much higher.

For Latter-day Saints it doubtless is, but should be better.

Utah, approximately 70 percent LDS, in 1980 saw 67.1 percent of its eligible voters go to the polls—fourth best among the fifty states. Minnesota was first, followed by Idaho and South Dakota. In 1976 Utah, with 69.4 percent, was second to Minnesota.

How should Jane Crezee vote in November?

That is something only she should decide.

But there are helpful guidelines to her and all voters—in the United States, Canada, and other democratic nations—in making choices.

Through the years, the First Presidency has provided wise counsel. Excerpts from a couple of their statements:

"The Church does not endorse candidates for office. However, we urge members as citizens to study carefully and prayerfully the candidates' records and their positions on issues. Similarly, we encourage members as citizens in supporting measures on the ballot which they feel will strengthen the community, state, and nation—morally, economically, and culturally." (April 24, 1976.)

"We as citizens cannot with conscience remain spectators when there are efforts to legalize immoral conduct such as gambling, obscenity, improper use of drugs, and dishonesty, nor when corrupt candidates seek office." (1974)

A former governor[1] (three terms) and ex-United States senator[2] (three terms) both put first on their list of qualities to look for in a candidate: integrity.

Both emphasized checking a candidate's qualifications especially for the office he or she seeks.

The former governor recommended voters read about candidates' backgrounds and positions on issues, and not rely so much on television appearances. "Some able candidates are less articulate," he said.

He could have cited James Madison, fourth president of the United States and "Father of the Constitution." Madison, if he lived today and people relied on his television performances, would probably have never been elected. He was only a wisp of a man physically and his voice was so weak it "prevented him from taking up a career as a minister." Washington Irving described him as "a withered little apple-John."

Yet few men have contributed as much in the molding and preserving of our form of government as Madison.

Deseret News Washington Bureau Chief Gordon Eliot White has been covering politics for twenty-eight years. For his superior journalism he has won such prestigious national honors as the Raymond Clapper Memorial Award for meritorious reporting, in 1978. In 1979 he was presented the National Press Club Award for top coverage of the executive branch of the federal government. His twin son and daughter voted the first time in 1982, and will vote in their first presidential election this year.

His advice to them:

"Look for an individual who is honest in what he tells the voters, one who does not say merely what the voters want to hear. A willingness to take an unpopular, but necessary position and stick to it is one of the attributes I value in a candidate."

All candidates on all levels of government should be reviewed and studied.

Yes, Jane Crezee has a priceless privilege, indeed a sacred duty, as a voter. She and her country will be better if she—and all others—vote prayerfully, and studiously.

Notes

1. Calvin L. Rampton, a Democrat.
2. Wallace F. Bennett, a Republican.

25

All Is Well!

She was tearful and fearful, this petite little curly-haired blond with blue eyes.

She hugged her father tightly as he carried her to the classroom.

Amy was five. This was her first day of school—kindergarten.

"Don't leave me," she pleaded. "Stay with me, Daddy."

In the fall of 1985, some 2.3 million youngsters across the United States, like Amy, will enter kindergarten.

Indeed, to many it will be entering the great unknown.

This year, approximately 870,000 Americans will receive a personal message that to most will likely bring sudden fear.

They will be told by a physician, or by a loved one for him, that they have cancer.

There will be other messages, events, and circumstances that may ignite fear or depression:

Loss of job.

Death of dear one.

An accident.

A "Dear John" letter.

A disappointment by an act of a companion or child.

A failure in business, a tryout, or contest.

Let us return to Amy:

The kindergarten teacher that day assembled her pupils, about twenty-five of them, around her on a big rug in the class-room.

Amy remained in the rear of the room, on her father's lap.

"We're so glad you're here, Amy," the teacher called.

No response.

The teacher led the tots in a song. Amy joined in.

The group sang about a hippopotamus.

The teacher asked Amy to hold a stuffed brown hippopota-mus with a yellow ribbon around its neck as the singing continued.

Amy held the stuffed animal.

"Can Daddy go to work now, Amy?" the teacher asked.

"Yes."

Fear had taken wings.

That teacher[1] for nineteen years has been instructing kinder-garteners—nearly a thousand of them.

"About half of them enter school fearful, in varying degrees," she said. "Fear goes when a child relates to someone he or she trusts."

An internationally eminent cancer surgeon[2] observed:

"Most patients on learning they have cancer are frightened— some terrified to a point of passing right out in the doctor's office."

Then he added, "But about 95 percent of them develop an acceptance of their malignancy. Then they cope with it admir-ably."

On the plain of Mamre the Amorite, the Lord spoke to Abraham. "Fear not, Abram: I am thy shield." (Genesis 15:1.)

Abraham put his trust in the Lord and walked nobly and courageously through many trials and triumphs.

Franklin D. Roosevelt rallied America in the Great Depres-sion in his 1933 inaugural address with:

"The only thing we have to fear is fear itself."

How do we conquer fear or avoid it?

The kindergarten teacher has found the answer in children: trust in someone.

"In God we trust" is inscribed in metal more than any other line in the United States. The message is on billions of our coins—a constant reminder to all who would fear.

What a moving expression of that trust in action are the words of William Clayton, a "Lancashire lad":

"And should we die before our journey's through,
Happy day! All is well!
We then are free from toil and sorrow too:
With the just we shall dwell."[3]

These words were penned on the trail near Locust Creek, Iowa, for the driven, homeless Mormon pioneers. The words are part of that great anthem known today as "Come, Come, Ye Saints."

In his diary on Wednesday, April 15, 1846, Clayton wrote:

"This morning I composed a new song—All Is Well."

In the hymn, each verse concludes with:

"All is well!"

It is a wonderful line to hum, even silently, when dark clouds gather, when weakening, soul-sapping fear moves to take command.

Notes

1. Mary Lynn Burningham.
2. Dr. Charles R. Smart.
3. *Hymns,* no. 13.

26

High Boots
and a Violin

Hans Christian Hansen was born in Copenhagen in 1806, when Norway was still under the Danish crown.

Hans Christian Andersen, the fairy tale author, had been born in Denmark the year before, and Napoleon was riding high across Europe.

Hans C. Hansen went to sea as a boy, and visited America several times. In Boston in 1842 at age thirty-five he was baptized into the Church. He joined the Saints in Nauvoo the following year. He became well-acquainted with the Prophet Joseph Smith and toiled on the Nauvoo Temple.

Hans baptized his brother, Peter Olsen Hansen, who later translated the Book of Mormon into Danish.

When the first company of Mormon Pioneers was organized at Winter Quarters in the spring of 1847, Hans was the only Scandinavian selected to make the trek. In the group under Brigham Young were 142 men, 3 women, and 2 boys.

Hans was in the thirteenth ten of the original trekkers, under Captain John Brown. Two of the three blacks in the first company were also in that group of ten: Hark Lay and Oscar Crosby.

Hans played the violin, and his string music often filled the night air around the campfire after the wagons had been formed in a circle.

Along the Platte River on the last day of April, Hans played his violin after dinner and the Pioneer men danced.

Almost a month later, along the Platte River near Chimney Rock, after chores were done, most of the high-booted pioneers whirled away in dance in the moonlight, probably with the Dane stroking the violin. The merriment continued until the bugle sounded its bed call at 9:00 P.M.

The following day was Sunday. As usual on the Sabbath, a Church service was held in the camp. Speakers included President Young and Elders Erastus Snow and George A. Smith, all of the Council of Twelve.

The Mormon pioneers under Brigham Young were rugged frontier-folk—tough, resilient colonizers who tamed the desert and built temples. The prime purpose of their efforts was to worship God through His restored gospel and to build His kingdom on earth.

Yet those doughty empire builders balanced their lives with organized fun and laughter. On the trail they danced to the beat of a violin. They chuckled also on the trek with mock trials, and celebrated the Fourth of July with "ice cream" made by George A. Smith, a young Apostle, with snow from a bank near the Green River, mixed with sugar.

The pioneers organized what today is the world-famed Salt Lake Mormon Tabernacle Choir the year they arrived in Salt Lake Valley. Soon after, a band was formed. Five years later, they built Social Hall, first playhouse west of the Missouri River. There was also an orchestra and brass band.

There was balance in Mormon pioneer life.

When President Lyndon B. Johnson in 1965 named John W. Gardner to his Cabinet, the president quoted from the educator's book *Excellence: Can We Be Equal and Excellent Too?*

"The society which scorns excellence in plumbing because plumbing is a humble activity and tolerates shoddiness in philosophy because it is an exalted activity will have neither good plumbing nor good philosophy. Neither its pipes nor its theories will hold water."

Balanced living usually begins at home. It did with Benjamin Franklin, who was described by one of his biographers[1] as "in himself a whole crowd of men."

In his autobiography, Franklin tells how his candlemaker father "strove to bring breadth and balance to his household." With thirteen Franklin children at the dinner table, Ben's father invited a "sensible friend or neighbor" to join them. Then the father would "start some ingenious or useful topic for discourse."

It is too often convenient to allow the good social life to crowd out caring for and about one's neighbor or the afflicted and needy.

It is often the choice to overly watch on television the show, the ball game, or the beauty pageant when the lawn needs grooming and the garden, weeding.

Sometimes piety crowds out good humor and lofty culture.

Hans Hansen and his violin. They remind us in this wondrous information, high-tech age that our Mormon pioneers had a balance we so much need today.

Notes

1. Donald Cubross Peattle in "Ben Franklin, Genius of Democracy," *Reader's Digest*, August, 1944.

27

Work with a Song

Disney is a happy name. It is linked with laughter, with lovable animals, light-hearted characters, and lofty cartoons.

In 1937, Walter Elias Disney, the Missouri farm boy who became the creator of all these, issued the first full-length cartoon motion picture: *Snow White and the Seven Dwarfs.* Based on a German folk tale, it became one of the most popular movies in history.

An endearing feature is a song sung by the seven dwarfs, "Whistle While You Work."[1]

As we think of Labor Day, it is good to remember that to Latter-day Saints one of the first and greatest blessings to mankind came when the Lord God spoke to Adam shortly before he was sent from the Garden of Eden to till the ground.

"In the sweat of thy face shalt thou eat bread." (Genesis 3:19.)

Some twenty-five hundred years later in a visitation with Moses on "an exceedingly high mountain," the Lord described His own works as "without end." He also spoke of "my work and my glory." (Moses 1:1, 4, 39.)

Indeed there is glory and joy in work. It is good to "whistle while you work."

Thomas Carlyle, the Scotsman who completely rewrote his *The French Revolution* after a friend's maid had accidentally burned the original manuscript, wrote:

"Work is a grand cure for all the maladies and miseries that ever beset mankind—honest work which you intend getting done."[2]

David Lynn Kenley is brown-eyed, auburn-haired, five feet, seven inches tall, and sixteen.

This year he was chosen over twelve hundred carriers of his newspaper for the Young Columbus Award, sponsored by *Parade* magazine—for superior work.

David this past school year was also president of the sophomore class, of the school's band (in which he plays the tuba "because my lips are not big enough for the trumpet"), of his seminary class, and of his teacher's quorum. He also runs the 100-yard dash and long jumps for the track team, and likes skiing and basketball. At fourteen he became an Eagle Scout.

The eldest son of six children, David has been the family's groundkeeper for six years. This includes raising pumpkins for Halloween.

He wants to attend BYU and study to be a newspaperman.

Loving to work works for David Kenley.

How did it all begin?

"My parents taught us to work and take responsibility since we were tots," David explains. "Work assignments began when we were only four years old—if nothing more than carrying out a bag of garbage."

David's father, Lynn G. Kenley, teaches ethics at a large juvenile detention center.

"My observation is that most all boys and girls who get into trouble with the law have not been taught to work or take responsibility," says Brother Kenley.

Otto von Bismarck, the Prussian statesman who united the German states into one empire during the 1860s and 1870s, said:

"To youth I have but three words of counsel—work, work, work."[3]

A few months ago the *Wall Street Journal* on its front page published a lengthy article datelined Convulsion Canyon, Utah.[4]

The article by Matt Moffet describes the operation of the coal mine there of Southern Utah Fuel Company (Sufco), owned by Coastal Corporation, Houston, Texas.

Of the mine in narrow, deep Convulsion Canyon, thirty miles east of Salina, Utah, and covered with scrub oak, long-needled pine, aspen, and Douglas fir, the *Journal* reports:

"They dig 2½ times more coal per man per day than is dug in the average underground coal mine in the U.S. . . .

"Sufco's Mormon miners and managers are certainly closeknit. They scrape elbows in the pit, rub elbows at the church banquet, and bang elbows at church-sponsored basketball games."

In charge of Coastal Corporation's mining and chemical operations, including the one at Convulsion Canyon, is Leo C. Smith, Coastal senior vice president. He is also president of the Houston Texas South Stake.

He credits a management philosophy with much of the success at Sufco and Coastal's other mining and chemical operations. He adds: "One day I realized that the most enlightened experts, leaders, and consultants were practicing and teaching the same principles put forth in Section 121 of the Doctrine and Covenants."

That section is in the form of "prayer and prophecies written by Joseph Smith the Prophet, while he was a prisoner in the jail at Liberty, Missouri, dated March 20, 1839." (Introduction to D&C 121.)

Labor Day. It is a time to remember:

Work and lead with a song in your heart!

Notes

1. Words by Larry Morey, music by Frank Churchill.
2. In *Inaugural Address,* Edinburgh, April 2, 1866.
3. *Sayings of Bismarck.*
4. *Wall Street Journal,* April 12, 1984.

28

Reflections
on the Nile

He is just ten, this Egyptian lad, with big, brown eyes and deep brown hair slightly curled. When he smiles, he displays beautiful snow-white teeth. His is a pug nose.

He sat there at the rear of the red and white sailboat working with his deft brown hands the ropes that control the rudder and gray canvas sail.

He wore a light green shirt with only one button fastened, revealing a bright emerald-green undershirt. His soiled blue pants had about a two-inch hole at one knee.

Like a cat, he climbed about the boat tugging and untying the various sized ropes.

His name is Ashraf and he helps his balding father, Ali Said, operate the sailboat on the blue-green Nile River in the heart of Cairo.

As Ashraf looks up from his ropes he sees a varied skyline: The blue, heavy-windowed Nile Hilton Hotel, minarets, sky-scrapers, palms, and television antennae.

As Ashraf sails up the Nile a few miles from Cairo, in the fading orange glow of an Egyptian sunset, his brown eyes can behold on the roads and highways two-wheeled carts pulled by skinny donkeys, camels, big diesel trucks, cars of all shapes and makes from around the world. He can see women in flowing black carrying baskets on their heads, and men in robe-like gowns irrigating the long rows of tall, verdant corn.

Ashraf's Egypt today is the patriarch among the nations. Approximately a thousand years before China's first dynasty was begun about 1700 B.C., Egyptians were building pyramids for burials, including the great Cheops Pyramid at Giza. The pyramid is the lone survivor of the Seven Wonders of the ancient world, covering an area equal to eight football fields.

More than a millennium before the Trojan War about 1200 B.C. Egyptian craftsmen were sculpting masterpieces in gold and stone.

Abraham found Egypt a great empire when he visited there some two thousand years before Christ. Joseph became the Pharaoh's ruler of mighty Egypt about two hundred years later. Moses, reared in a royal household on the Nile, led the Israelites from Egypt's bondage.

This was about the time of one of Egypt's best remembered, if not greatest, monarchs: Ramses II. He reigned sixty-seven years, erecting spectatular statues to himself. Two of them, seated figures, thrill visitors to Egypt today. They rise seventy-six feet high at Luxor, up the Nile 416 miles from Cairo.

Some 1,250 years after Ramses II was building these and other magnificent monuments to himself and his gods, a couple and infant Child entered Egypt. They were Joseph and Mary and Son of Nazareth in Galilee of Palestine, about three hundred miles northeast of the Nile delta.

The three remained in Egypt until the death of wicked Herod the Great.

Yes, no nation has the long-lasting splendor of Egypt's past — this Egypt of Ashraf, the smiling boat boy.

Egypt's ancient kings and queens sought immortality more than anything else.

They built awesome pyramids and carved out palatial caverns for their burials. Into these sanctums they poured piles of precious jewelry, furniture, ornaments, weapons, and tools.

"They believed with deep conviction that you *can* take it with you," wrote Alice J. Hall in her graphic portrayal of ancient Egypt in *National Geographic*.[1]

But their tombs and temples were plundered by robbers and probed by archaeologists.

The greatest treasure ever found in Egypt was discovered in 1922: the hidden tomb of the boy-king Tutankhamen (King Tut). Nearly five thousand dazzling items came from his shrine. His remains were found in a mummiform coffin of solid gold weighing 2,448 pounds.

Mary, the mother of Jesus, no doubt told Him as a boy something of the splendor of this kingdom along the Nile where He lived for a short time as a babe.

It could be He reflected on all this when He declared in a far more meaningful masterpiece than all the glittering gold creations of Egypt's pharaohs seeking life everlasting—the Sermon on the Mount:

"Lay not up for yourselves treasures upon earth, where moth and rust doth corrupt, and where thieves break through and steal:

"But lay up for yourselves treasures in heaven. . . .

"But seek ye first the kingdom of God, and his righteousness." (Matthew 6:19–20, 33.)

That is a timeless message for Ashraf, pulling ropes on the Nile today. And for people everywhere in this the most wondrous and challenging age of all history.

———————————

Notes

1. Cover feature, March 1977.

29

Multiplying Yourself

The pinstriped suit you could be wearing—men's or women's—may have been made in Korea. Your wristwatch may have come from a mountain-rimmed city in Japan—Matsumoto. If yours is a top-quality sweater, it could have been produced in Scotland or Ireland.

Your shoes may be Italian made, and your handkerchief could have come from Hong Kong, the Philippines, or Taiwan.

As the world draws closer through transportation and communications, so does it become more competitive. Automobile workers in Detroit realize today they are competing with car makers in Stuttgart and Nagoya.

Thus the business of ably delegating becomes more and more important—getting superior results with less cost.

So it is in the home.

Fifty-two percent of America's women were employed in 1980, and the percentage is rising. Forty-six percent of women with children under six years old are employed. One of three U.S. women does not have a male to provide support. From 1970 to 1982 the number of families maintained by women alone increased more than 51 percent to 9.4 million.

These are not happy figures, but they underline the need for better delegating at home.

The Church operates through delegated authority and action.

How do you delegate better?

Jesus is the master. Consider these lessons on delegating from His earthly ministry:

1. *In delegating, Jesus did not make the assignment sound easy, but He made it ring with excitement and challenge.*

He called the fishermen brothers, Peter and Andrew, to a demanding work that was to bring them ridicule, and, according to tradition, even martyrdom.

But it was to be gloriously important and exciting work, and the Master gave it that sound.

"I will make you to become fishers of men," he told them. (Mark 1:17.)

2. *At the outset Jesus instructed those delegated in their duties.*

In *Jesus the Christ* Elder James E. Talmage wrote:

"For a season following their ordination the apostles remained with Jesus, being specially trained and instructed by Him for the work then before them."[1]

3. *Jesus gave those He delegated His confidence as His Father had given Him.*

On at least four occasions, the Father introduced Him: "This is my beloved Son, in whom I am well pleased." This was at the baptism of Jesus (Matthew 3:17), the Transfiguration (2 Peter 1:17), to the Nephites around the temple in the land Bountiful (3 Nephi 11:7), and at the first vision to the Prophet Joseph Smith (Joseph Smith—History 1:17).

Jesus called His Apostles "friends." He told them He loved them as His Father loved Him. He washed their feet.

4. *Jesus gave to those He called His loyalty, and He expected their loyalty in return.*

Following the Last Supper, Jesus assured the Eleven: "I will not leave you comfortless." (John 14:18.)

5. *Jesus expected much from those delegated.*

To the Eleven, shortly before His ascension, He gave them a global charge:

"Go ye into all the world, and preach the gospel to every creature." (Mark 16:15.)

6. *Jesus seemed to invite feedback from those assigned.*

Mark records:

"And the apostles gathered themselves together unto Jesus, and told him all things, both what they had done, and what they had taught." (Mark 6:30.)

7. *Jesus taught that he who leads should follow the progress of those delegated, giving praise and reproof in a spirit of love.*

In His parable of the talents the Master said:

"Well done, thou good and faithful servant: thou hast been faithful over a few things, I will make thee ruler over many things: enter thou into the joy of thy lord." (Matthew 25:21.)

8. *Jesus demonstrated the power that comes through praying to the Father before making assignments.*

The night before the morn on which Jesus called and ordained His Twelve, in a secluded mountain place He "continued all night in prayer to God." (Luke 6:12.)

Someone said: "Effective management is the art of multiplying yourself through others."

How masterfully the Prince of Peace, the supreme Delegant, demonstrated that truth!

Notes

1. Talmage, James E., *Jesus the Christ*, 3rd ed. (Salt Lake City, Utah: The Church of Jesus Christ of Latter-day Saints, 1916), p. 228.

30

Discovery
Before Israel

Several thousand Latter-day Saints this year are visiting the Holy Land.

Among them is Renate Hasse Voss (pronounced Re-*not*-eh *Hoss*-eh *Voss*). Renate is fortyish, a mother of six. She is a petite five feet one-half inch tall, with honey-hued hair, light blue eyes, and a cream-colored complexion.

She was born during World War II in Scholochau in eastern Germany (now part of Poland) in an area of small lakes and pine forests, some thirty miles south of the Baltic Sea.

The Hasse family struggled westward across Germany during the war, ahead of the invading Soviet army. The Hasses settled in Solingen, a steel products manufacturing city amid the rolling, forested hills about twenty-five miles southeast of Dusseldorf.

There in Solingen, when Renate was twenty-one, she joined the Church, the only one of her family of seven. After serving a mission in England, she emigrated to the United States. There she married black-haired, husky Howard L. Voss[1], former missionary to Germany. Today he is a successful computer programmer-salesman.

With a family group, Renate and Howard Voss a few weeks ago toured Israel.

On a calm summer morning with a faded full moon still in the cloudless sky, they bused from walled Jerusalem some six miles to a sleepy little city on a hill with stone, flat-roofed homes, many gray or cream-colored.

This was Bethlehem, birthplace of Jesus.

They admired valleys that not long ago were arid, now fruited with plump yellow-green grapes and sweet-tasting apples, pears, plums, and peaches. Where Jesus taught the multitudes and healed the halt and blind, they saw vast green stretches of growing cotton and groves of bananas, oranges, and avocados.

There was a strong wind as Renate's group sat on a stone-stepped hillside overlooking a misty Sea of Galilee. Its waters are still worked by fishermen.

On this hillside, today called the Mount of the Beatitudes, near Capernaum, home of Peter, the group sat reflectively. They took turns reading the Sermon on the Mount. A family prayer was spoken by a silver-haired father who also blessed his kin.

Renate learned that Israel's Jewish population today is drawn from 102 countries speaking seventy different languages. (Some cities, such as Nazareth, remain mostly Arab.)

Gratefully, the group gathered by gnarled olive trees, said to be eighteen hundred years old, near the foot of the Mount of Olives. Here, it was explained, is the likely site of Gethsemane. Together they read Mark's account.

The crowning experience in Israel for the family was in a garden where there is an ancient tomb carved out of a stone-ribbed eminence in Jerusalem. Increasingly there is evidence that here is where the supreme event of the Savior's earthly life occurred: the Resurrection.

There is no church or shrine marking this place—only a garden. It is shady with towering, bushy pines and olive, mustard, lemon, pomegranate, and other trees. There are pink roses, too, and red geraniums, cactus plants, and others.

In a leafy nook in this garden, the family assembled on benches: some stone, some wood.

Together they sang "I Know That My Redeemer Lives" and "I

Need Thee Every Hour." Several took turns reading John 20, describing that glorious first Easter morn, including the risen Christ's greeting to Mary Magdalene.

In the chapter the group also read of doubting Thomas. Jesus asked Thomas: "Reach hither thy finger, and behold my hands."

A believing Thomas then exclaimed: "My Lord and my God."

Jesus responded:

"Thomas, because thou hast seen me, thou hast believed: blessed are they that have not seen, and yet have believed." (John 20:27–29.)

With these telling lines came a thought to one of the group. He discussed it with Renate.

They agreed that glowing inspiration, far greater than words can describe, can come through following the footsteps of the Master in today's Israel.

But they also agreed an even greater closeness to the Redeemer can come without visiting the Holy Land.

"When the missionaries in Germany asked me to read the Book of Mormon, they suggested I start not at the beginning of the book, but with Third Nephi," Renate recalled. "There I read of the glory of the resurrected Lord's ministry among His 'other sheep.' In Germany I found a deep, new relationship with the Savior, one that continues to this day."

Jesus, as He spoke to Thomas, indeed could have been also talking of countless Saints who have truly discovered Him to a point of commitment—as did a blue-eyed young woman in Germany one score four years ago: "Blessed are they that have not seen, and yet have believed." (John 20:29.)

———————

Notes

1. Sandy 40th Ward, Utah Alta View Stake.

31

"He Careth for You"

In Houston, Texas, a young Latter-day Saint woman who is a clothing store chain executive recently picked up her needle and thread.

But it was not to sew a new dress design, nor to fasten back a fallen button.

In her little single-story, reddish-orange brick apartment the brown-haired, blue-eyed woman began a needlepoint piece, about ten inches wide by eight inches.

After some four weeks, the needlepoint was finished. On a cream-colored background she had stitched with maroon, yarn-like thread a message, not original with her but one she treasured. Around the saying, she had sewn an attractive border in dark and light blue.

The message:

> *Nobody cares how*
> *much you know*
> *until they know*
> *how much you care.*

Then she carefully placed the finished needlepoint in an attractive oak frame. It was mailed as a gift to her father some thirteen hundred miles away.

To the divided Saints in ancient Corinth, Greece, Paul wrote some of his most meaningful and eloquent words of wisdom. He counseled them to be a united body, urging them to "care one for another." (1 Corinthians 12:25.) With that statement on caring, he followed with his timeless discourse on charity.

London-born, slender Pamela Atkinson has been a nurse and a supervisor of nurses in various parts of the world, including Thursday Island. It is a speck on the map, off the tip of Australia's horn, some three hundred miles from Papua, New Guinea.

Pamela has seen a lot of heroic caring in and out of hospital rooms—including Australian Aborigines, New Guineans, British, Americans, and others.

Some of her recent observations:

A fifty-four-year-old, retarded man came this year to the hospital[1] where she is assistant administrator. He had cancer of the bowels. After he was discharged from the hospital, nurses phoned him daily. More than that, they invited him back to the hospital—for a birthday party. They presented him a cake with pink and white icing, inscribed "Happy Birthday." They gave him stuffed animals, books and homemade cookies. The calls to his home continued until two days before his death.

A fifty-six-year-old cancer patient, paralyzed from the waist down, lived alone. Her closest friend was her cat. Nurses arranged for the pet to visit her in the hospital. Then they presented her a stuffed cat to have at her side during her difficult hospital stay.

The mother[2] of a nineteen-year-old son with a critical respiratory disease came with him to the hospital. For the last month of his life she was at his side night and day. That was two years ago. She has continued to come to the hospital faithfully—to comfort others with a loved one critically ill.

William Gilmore Simms, a nineteenth-century American novelist and poet, wrote:

"Our cares are the mothers not only of our charities and virtues, but of our best joys, and most cheering and enduring pleasures."

One of the most popular nonfiction books in America during 1982—84 is *In Search of Excellence: Lessons from America's Best-run Companies,* by Thomas J. Peters and Robert H. Waterman, Jr.

In the acknowledgements the authors describe the volume: "This book, if anything, is about caring and commitment."

Throughout the text they stress that the best-run businesses are those that *care—about people.*

A key section of the book begins telling about car salesman Joe Girard. "He sold more new cars and trucks for eleven years running, than any other human being."

Joe's secret? To quote him:

"I . . . believe the sale really begins *after* the sale—not before."

He sends thank-you notes. "I send out over 13,000 cards every month."

A gimmick? The authors write:

"But like the top companies, Joe seems genuinely *to care.*" When something goes wrong with a customer's car Joe feels "hurt for him"—and acts and helps accordingly.

The book tells how the successful business giants like IBM, Disney, Frito-Lay, Marriott, and 3M train their personnel to be sincerely *caring,* like Joe.

Caring about people is as simple, warm, homey, and tender as a needle and thread in loving hands.

But it is also so powerful, so Godlike.

It was Peter, the Big Fisherman and first Apostle, who wrote of the Lord: "He careth for you." (1 Peter 5:7.)

Notes

    1. LDS Hospital.

    2. Mrs. L. Burke (Mildred) Tangren.

32

Man with a Mission

The year was 1451. The place was Genoa. It was a seacoast city-state tucked high in the northwest corner of the Italian boot. Ten years earlier, Joan of Arc, a peasant girl who had led the French army to victory over the British at Orleans, was burned at the stake. A year later, the great artist-inventor, Leonardo da Vinci, was to be born some 150 miles from Genoa, near Florence.

In this year, 1451, a son was born to a Genoa wool weaver. The child's mother was a daughter of a wool weaver.

But the boy, who helped his father at the loom, longed to be a seaman.

His name was Christopher Columbus.

To sea he did indeed go.

On October 12, 1492, near his forty-first birthday anniversary, Columbus landed in the New World—discoverer of America. (His actual birth date is not known, but was "sometime between August 25 and the end of October, 1451.")

On Monday, October 8, 1984, the United States commemorated Columbus Day. Until 1971 it was celebrated October 12, but since, on the second Monday of October. Many Latin American countries honor Columbus annually on October 12.

When Columbus discovered America at age forty-one he was white-haired. In his younger years his hair was red. He was tall, well-built, with a lank face and high cheekbones. He was ruddy-faced, blue-eyed, hawk-nosed.

Bartolme de Las Casas, who saw Columbus eight years after his first voyage to the New World, was son and nephew of two shipmates of Columbus. Las Casas wrote a scholarly book on the discovery of America, *Historia de las Indias,* completed in 1563. In it he writes of Columbus:

"He was serious in moderation, affable with strangers, and with members of his household gentle and pleasant . . . a person of great state and authority and worthy of all reverence." He also described Columbus as eloquent and boastful in his negotiations . . . moderate in eating, drinking, clothing and footwear . . . [who] spoke cheerfully in familiar conversation, or with indignation when he gave reproof."

Samuel Eliot Morison, in his Pulitzer Prize-winning biography of Columbus, *Admiral of the Ocean Sea* (1942), wrote:

"Columbus was a Man with a Mission, and such men are apt to be unreasonable and even disagreeable to those who cannot see the mission. . . .

"He was a Man alone with God against human stupidity and depravity, against greedy conquistadors, cowardly seamen, even against nature and the sea. . . .

"Always with God . . . there can be no doubt that the faith of Columbus was genuine and sincere. . . . It gave him confidence in his destiny."

Morison described this incident on the second voyage of Columbus:

Along the Jamaica coast, Columbus was praying in his cabin. A native chief "with a large retinue" boarded the ship. Undoubtedly there was excitement on deck, "but none of the loud talking and tumult disturbed the Admiral's prayers, and he finished his devotions with no suspicion that anything unusual was going on."

Homeward bound on his discovery voyage, near the Azores, Columbus wrote a letter. It was no doubt intended for Spain's King Ferdinand and Queen Isabella, who financed the voyage.

Columbus began the letter: "Knowing the pleasure you will

receive in hearing of the great victory which Our Lord has granted me in my voyage."

He described the islands he discovered. There were tall mountains covered with lofty trees, both flowered and fruited. Palms and pines reached high. There were beautiful, warbling birds, lovely harbors, lush meadows, and honey bees. The natives were gentle, long-haired, and "use bows and arrows."

The Admiral concluded his letter: "This is ever-certain, that God grants to those that walk in His ways, the performance of things which seem impossible. . . .

". . . all Christendom should rejoice, and give solemn thanks to the holy Trinity. . . ."

Such was the man Columbus and his mission, about whom a prophet in ancient America wrote some two thousand years before.

Recorded Nephi, the mighty prophet-leader:

"And I looked and beheld a man among the Gentiles, who was separated from the seed of my brethren by the many waters; and I beheld the Spirit of God, that it came down and wrought upon the man; and he went forth upon the many waters, even unto the seed of my brethren, who were in the promised land." (1 Nephi 13:12.)

33

Seeds of Sinister Sex

From Providence, Rhode Island, last spring came a shocking Associated Press report about a Pawtucket boy described as "non-violent and 'pint-sized at about four feet tall.' "

The head of the attorney general's juvenile prosecution unit, Jack McMahon, described the incident as "a good kid gone awry." Mr. McMahon added:

"The kid unfortunately watched too much stuff on TV."

The Associated Press story began: "A 12-year-old boy was arraigned Tuesday on charges that he sexually assaulted a girl on a pool table while other children watched, and officials said he may have taken the idea from watching Big Dan's rape trial on television."

A sordid story—one good people do not like to think or talk about.

But incidents like that are increasing at an alarming rate. Approximately 95,000 cases of sexual abuse to children were reported in the United States in 1982, according to the National Center for Child Abuse and Neglect, Washington, D.C. The number this year is expected to reach between 100,000 and 300,000.

Authorities estimate 85 percent are incest related—relatives involved.

In the past fifty years the rape rate in the United States has risen seven times. And authorities say only one in four attempted or actual rapes is reported to police.

What is causing this growing plague that so often strikes crushingly on innocent children and women?

Specialists say there are a number of contributing causes. A big one is sex encounters portrayed on TV.

Approximately 30 percent of the nation's homes now have cable TV. Expected by the end of the 1980s: close to 80 percent.

There is much on cable TV that is wholesome and uplifting: symphony music, a broad selection of professional and college sports, discussions on important issues of the day, documentaries and travelogues.

But cable TV is not regulated by the Federal Communications Commission as is commercial television.

And that is where the "peddlers of porn"—a $7 billion-a-year business in the USA—bring explicit sex into the livingroom through cable TV.

Cable TV shows "hard R" motion pictures that commercial television stations show only at the peril of losing their licenses.

With no such restrictions, cable TV is growing increasingly obscene. Some cable TV channels in the U.S. are "broadcasting the roughest kind of hard core pornography," according to Victor L. Cline, Ph.D., one of the nation's top authorities on the subject.

HBO network cable TV programs such movies as *The Blue Lagoon, Tattoo, Talking Sex,* and *Private Lessons,* displaying "provocative nudity, simulated sexual intercourse, and offensive language."

Private Lessons, for example, is the story of a fourteen-year-old boy being seduced by an attractive, unrestrained housekeeper.

In an address at the National Catholic Conference on the Illegal Sex Industry, in New York on June 2, 1984, Dr. Cline described results of studies on the influence on people's behavior of media (such as cable TV) portrayals. In summary, he said:

They (media presentations on sex and violence) stimulate and arouse aggressive and sexual feelings—especially in males.

"They show or instruct in detail *how* to do the acts. . . .

"When seen frequently enough (they) have a desensitization effect that reduces feelings of conscience, guilt, inhibitions, or inner controls. . . .

"There is increased likelihood the individual will act out what he has witnessed."

All of this reaffirms the words of wisdom of Ralph Waldo Emerson, great American essayist: "Thought is the seed of action."[1]

And of the brilliant English poet, Percy Bysshe Shelley: "Strange thoughts beget strange deeds."[2]

There are those who say there should be no legal restraints on cable TV, that to do so would violate the First Amendment.

The Supreme Court has ruled First Amendment rights to free speech do not protect the obscene.

Also, it is not reasonable to think that James Madison, "the Father of the Constitution," intended to protect the smut on cable TV that is not shown on commercial television.

Of Madison, his close friend Thomas Jefferson wrote:

A man of "pure and spotless virtue which no calumny has ever attempted to sully."[3]

As concerned, caring citizens, Latter-day Saints will want to let their voices be heard relative to putting the same restraints on cable TV that apply to commercial TV regarding indecency: "seeds of sinister sex."

Notes

1. *Essays, First Series: Spiritual Laws.*
2. *The Cinci,* act 4, scene 4, 1.
3. Padover, Saul K., *The Complete Madison,* p. 3.

34

His First in the Tabernacle

There he sat on the light brown wood bench with a curved back and a red cushion on the seat, on the front row. His deep maroon shoes rested on the light red carpet. His blond head on his short, slim frame was erect. His light blue eyes focused on the walnut podium. It was banked in front by three huge bouquets of chrysanthemums—deep reds, glowing yellows, and bright blooms of orange. Fringing the bottom of the bouquets were stems of big, bright leaves.

Peter Vidmar, 1984 Olympic gold medalist (two golds plus a silver) in gymnastics, was attending his first session of general conference in the vast, oval-domed Salt Lake Tabernacle.

It was a glorious October day. The towering Rockies rimming Salt Lake Valley were aglow with brilliant autumn colors matching the chrysanthemums inside.

Peter had attended general conferences before: by radio in his student ward meeting place at the University of California at Los Angeles, or by satellite in his Los Angeles stake center. But never before in person on Temple Square.

In the lapel of his dark blue coat was a small metal Nissen pin. It was awarded him in 1983 as America's number one collegiate gymnast.

His dark blue tie was decorated with the small green figures of flying mallards.

"Donna gave me this tie because she knows I like ducks," Peter said. Donna, his brown-haired wife, sat at his side in the Tabernacle.

Peter had baptized her into the Church three years ago, when both were UCLA gymnasts. They were married in the Los Angeles Temple in the summer of 1983.

Peter and Donna listened intently as President Gordon B. Hinckley of the First Presidency opened the conference with a welcome. He announced that assembled Church members were witnessing this session by satellite in over nine hundred stake centers across the United States and Canada.

President Hinckley presented the name of Elder Marion D. Hanks, a General Authority for thirty-one years, as a new member of the Presidency of the First Quorum of the Seventy.

Peter and Donna also saw three new members of the First Quorum of the Seventy take their places in the red upholstered seats on the stand immediately in front of the Vidmars, after President Hinckley had presented their names:

Elder John Sonnenberg of Chicago, Illinois.

Elder F. Arthur Kay of Seattle, Washington.

Elder Keith Wilson Wilcox of Ogden, Utah.

Peter and Donna heard President Ezra Taft Benson speak powerfully on the Book of Mormon.

Also, Elder Neal A. Maxwell described how the Church is moving from obscurity to visibility; and Elder M. Russell Ballard spoke on the challenges and opportunities of missionary work. "More people are born in one day than are baptized into the Church in one year," Elder Ballard said.

Peter must have reflected there in the Tabernacle on his own experiences at UCLA when he refused the gymnast coach's request to work out on Sunday—when Elder L. Tom Perry in that first session talked about observing the Sabbath.

Peter heard at that session an Apostle give his first general conference address. He is Elder Dallin H. Oaks.

After the meeting, Peter was asked his impressions of that first conference session for him in the Tabernacle.

"It has been a fantastic experience," he replied. "Donna and I have so much wanted to someday attend a conference here.

"I was impressed by all the talks," he continued. "But what really moved me were the words of Elder Oaks. Remember how he said, 'Serve one another for the highest and best reason, the pure love of Christ'?

"I liked that," said Peter soberly. He has been a stake missionary for a year and a half.

Others were there at Temple Square for a heart-warming general conference. On the grounds between meetings were Japanese members, dark-suited and with cameras; Mexicans with colorful shawls; big and brown-skinned Tongans and Samoans; black-haired Chileans and Brazilians; and others from far and near.

There were conference visitors, too, who were not members of the Church. Among them were sixtyish Barbara and F. Vincent Regan of Toronto. He directs one of North America's big truck lines and is also a prominent Canadian attorney.

After attending the Sunday morning session and watching President Spencer W. Kimball join with the congregation in singing "I Am a Child of God," Mrs. Regan, a Catholic, said: "Inspirational!"

It was a mighty two-day meeting of a growing worldwide Church tackling the challenges of a new visibility.

Donna and Peter Vidmar and more than a million other members who watched or listened were no doubt stirred by the words of Elder Bruce R. McConkie in the concluding session:

"The Church is like a great caravan—organized, prepared, following an appointed course. . . .

"What does it matter if a few barking dogs snap at the heels of the weary travellers? . . . The caravan moves on."

35

Goodly Gathering Place

Hebron today is a city of about forty thousand people nestled amid low hills twenty-three miles south of Jerusalem in Israel and about the same distance west of the Dead Sea.

Hebron is a garden city of winding, narrow roads. In and around the city are well-groomed vineyards, heavy in the late summer with huge clusters of yellow-green grapes. There are also smiling patches of melons, and orchards, and row crops. Many of the farms are bordered with low, gray stone walls.

Hebron is one of the oldest cities of the world. After his return from Egypt, Abraham settled "in the plain of Mamre, which is in Hebron, and built there an altar unto the Lord." (Genesis 13:18.)

That was approximately four thousand years ago.

Abraham's wife Sarah died at Hebron, aged 127 years.

Abraham apparently wanted Hebron to be a gathering place for his family, dead as well as living.

From the sons of Heth, Abraham at Hebron purchased for four hundred shekels the field of Machpelah with its cave. There, Abraham said, he would "bury [my] dead." (Genesis 23:11.)

In the cave at Hebron, Abraham buried Sarah.

Forty-eight years later, Abraham was buried there.

Isaac, at 180 years, "was gathered unto his people," and buried by his sons Esau and Jacob—also in the cave at Hebron.

As he neared his sundown in Egypt, Jacob called his sons together and blessed each. Then he asked his sons to bury him, not in Egypt where he had resided seventeen years, but "with my fathers in the cave" at Hebron. (Genesis 49:29.)

After seventy days of mourning by the Egyptians, Joseph, the pharaoh's ruler of the land, led the procession with Jacob's remains to Canaan. There were chariots and horsemen, the pharaoh's elders and "all the elders of the land of Egypt." It was "a very great company," including Jacob's family except "their little ones." (Genesis 50:7—9.) The journey was some six hundred miles to the burial place and return.

Jacob was buried at Hebron with his wife Leah, Abraham and Sarah, Isaac and Rebekah.

Hebron had been a family gathering place for the living. It was also a family gathering place to mourn and bury the dead.

There are many homes today that are unifying places of gathering.

"His home is not only a place where his family, including his brother's family, comes together often—but his home is also a wonderful gathering place for his children's friends."

That is how a friend of his daughter Michelle describes the home of Reed Fogg, a bone surgeon who serves in a stake presidency.[1]

The teen friend continues:

"We girls always feel so welcome at his home. When a group of us go there to watch TV, he will fix a bowl of popcorn for us. He visits with us as though he is one of us.

"Recently when some of us girls had a slumber party at a mountain retreat, he surprised us by driving to the place early in the morning and fixing breakfast, including pancakes with strawberries and whipped cream."

A couple, parents of seven adult children, several times a year gather their children, their spouses, and grandchildren to their home for a cookout and games. In addition, on the evening of the first Sunday of each month they gather with their children and spouses for a family prayer, gospel or other uplifting discussion, and refreshments. Generally a family member leads the discussion, but a guest speaker may be invited.

Faithful holding of daily family prayers and weekly family home evening is a powerful pillar in making a blessed gathering place for many LDS homes.

A recent report from the U.S. Census Bureau shows 62 percent of the nation's married couples have two incomes, up from 40 percent in 1960, and with a prediction of 80 percent by the year 2000.

With this outside involvement, it is so easy to make of the evening meal a "pit stop" or "TV snack."

But dinner *can* be a goodly gathering time.

Wrote Henry Wadsworth Longfellow, father of six and devoted family man and only American poet honored with a bust in London's Westminster Abbey:

A holy family, that make

Each meal a Supper of the Lord.[2]

Longfellow seemed to make of his shuttered, frame home in Cambridge, Massachusetts, a joyous family gathering place— truly a modern Hebron.

Of your home, you can too!

Notes

1. Salt Lake Mount Olympus North Stake.

2. *The Golden Legend,* part 1.

36

Song of the Righteous

Her name was Christine Rautenbach, an attractive South African young woman with blue-gray eyes, brown hair, and a song in her heart. She was the daughter of a medical practitioner.

At twenty-five she was on her way to Vienna to further her studies in singing. In South Africa, she had completed five years of university study in fine arts.

She had worked hard to finance her studies in Europe. In her native Bloemfontein she had taught at a high school in the mornings, and conducted art classes in the afternoons and evenings at a technical college.

To bring more needed funds, she had also designed ten floats for a street pageant during the area's centennial celebrations. (Bloemfontein is capital of Orange Free State, one of South Africa's four provinces. Orange Free State became a republic in 1854.)

Vienna had much appeal for the South African songstress. In Vienna were famed opera houses, a great symphony, and the Academy of Music. The city on the Danube, too, had been the home of great composers: Beethoven, Brahms, Haydn, Mozart, Schubert, and the Strausses.

Studying under a Vienna tutor, Christine, however, became discouraged. Her progress was slow.

She prayed for guidance.

Two Latter-day Saint missionaries came to her door.

"My singing progressed rapidly after I discovered a new set of values," she said.

"On an icy cold day," October 10, 1955, Christine was baptized in what Johann Strauss, Jr., called "the beautiful blue Danube."

Two years after her return to South Africa, she married a law student, Charl H. du Plessis. Just over a year later, he joined the Church.

So he could gain experience in practicing law, the couple moved to a gold-mining town near Johannesburg: Krugersdorp. (South Africa has long yielded most of the world's gold.)

There was a small branch of the Church in Krugersdorp, with approximately thirty-five members attending the meetings in a rented hall.

Christine was asked to organize and direct a branch choir. The miners, their wives, and others knew little about music. There was a small, poorly tuned piano for accompaniment.

But a choir was organized, with twelve branch members, or fewer, participating. They began learning such hymns as "The Lord Is My Shepherd," "Though Deepening Trials," and "O My Father."

The little choir sang joyously.

Four sons were born to Christine and Charl. His work took them to other cities. Christine organized and directed other branch choirs, sometimes with only three singers.

They eventually settled in Pretoria, a city with over a half million population. The Pretoria Deseret Ward meetinghouse today has four pianos and an organ.

For twenty-nine years after her baptism Christine du Plessis conducted branch and ward choirs and Relief Society and Primary choruses. Her beautiful soprano voice also provided solos at Church services.

Two of her four sons have served full-time missions for the Church. A third son is now in the field. A fourth son is planning for a mission. One son, his mission completed, is now a student at Brigham Young University.

Christine has had her "Gethsemanes," including a divorce.

But Christine's leadership with Church choirs and choruses continues. She knows that the Lord "delighteth in the song of the heart." (D&C 25:12.)

Music plays a major role in sacrament and other meetings in the more than fourteen thousand wards and branches of the Church around the world.

Music usually lifts hearts and turns thoughts heavenward even more reverently when there is the togetherness of a choir such as those Christine de Plessis has nurtured and led.

Surely the Lord would say of her and countless other choir leaders like her: "The song of the righteous is a prayer unto me." (D&C 25:12.)

37

Silver and Green: Rich Blend

In the Spanish I class of some twenty students in Los Angeles Community College twice each week sits a wiry, silver-haired sixty-eight-year-old.

He is J. Robert Vaughan, senior member of a prominent Los Angeles law firm. He recently retired as chief executive officer of Knudsen Corporation, California's largest dairy foods processor and distributor.

The Spanish class consists of mostly low income, young students, including blacks and Hispanics. The teacher is a young Mexican educated in Columbia.

Why is Bob Vaughan taking time out from law practice for the course?

"I took six years of Latin in college," he explained. "Spanish is a phonetic language, and I thought it would be good to really learn to speak and read a foreign language.

"Besides, I enjoy mixing with young people," he continued. "We need to keep in touch with youth."

And youth's lives will be more abundant through mixing with the wisdom and stability of age!

Perhaps the most brilliant, versatile mind to ever occupy the White House was the former Virginia farmboy, fatherless at fourteen: Thomas Jefferson.

When shy, auburn-haired Jefferson at sixteen entered William and Mary College at Williamsburg he soon struck up an acquaintance with three distinguished men: George Wythe, an astute attorney; William Small, professor of mathematics at the college; and Francis Fauquier, Virginia's able and popular governor.

The four met often in the evening at the governor's mansion "talking and playing chamber music," with Jefferson stroking the violin.

Of this blending of youth with age at the governor's mansion, Jefferson later wrote:

"I have heard more good sense, more rational and philosophical conversations, than all my life besides. They were truly Attic (meaning the pure, refined and classical tone of Attica or Athens) societies."[1]

Today, the numbers of youth continue to grow. So do the ranks of the silver-haired. Notes *John Naisbitt's Trend Letter:*

"Older people are receiving more attention, from both the business and political worlds, simply because they're the fastest-growing segment of the population. The number of Americans sixty-five years or older is now growing twice as fast as the population as a whole.

"Even the 'oldest old,' Americans eighty-five years or more, exceed 2.3 million. By the year 2000, only fifteen years away, the number will more than double, to 5.4 million . . . and each day an average of thirty Americans become one hundred years old."[2]

Recently at a ward overnight hike into the oaks, maples, and pines of the high Rockies, boys, fathers, and grandfathers clustered around a campfire. While some toasted marshmallows, all joined in a song led spontaneously by Arlo Evans, a seven-year-old, brown-eyed boy with a blue wool pullover cap on his head.

All trilled merrily, following the boy, a line at a time, as the words told of a grizzly bear and a man in a tree.

At the same campfire, in the chill of the autumn air, boys sat bug-eyed as a seventyish high priest told of the harrowing experience of a pioneer hunter with a grizzly.

There are so many opportunities in the Church for that rich blending of youth with age.

The supreme model of the high rewards of the mixing of youth and age occurred in Jerusalem's temple. To Jerusalem, Joseph and Mary had brought the twelve-year-old Jesus for the feast of the Passover and to be presented in the temple. Returning to Nazareth in a caravan, the earthly parents of Jesus discovered Him missing. "After three days they found him in the temple, sitting in the midst of doctors, both hearing them, and asking them questions." (Luke 2:46.)

The following is all the scriptures recorded of Jesus during the next eighteen years of His life:

"And Jesus increased in wisdom and stature, and in favour with God and man." (Luke 2:52.)

Certainly the wise men in the temple were enriched through those discussions with the Boy. And He through their mature wisdom.

In this the era of wondrous strides in communications, youth could heed the lines of John Townsend Trowbridge, American novelist and poet (1827–1916):

> With years a richer life begins,
> The spirit mellows:
> Ripe age gives tone to violins. . . .[3]

And the older set could smile on the words of George Bernard Shaw, the twinkling Irish playwright (1856–1950):

"Youth is a wonderful thing. What a crime to waste it on children."[4]

A rich blend: mixing of the green of youth and the silver of age. It should occur more often.

Notes

1. *Thomas Jefferson, a Biography In His Own Words*, Joseph L. Gardner, ed. (Newsweek Books, New York, 1974), p. 22.

2. Sept. 20, 1984.

3. *Three Works.*

4. *The New Dictionary of Thoughts* (New York, Doubleday, 1977), p. 746.

38

The Grateful Samaritan

Simi Valley is a fast growing "bedroom" city of some eighty thousand people. It is situated amid huge orange and walnut groves midway between Los Angeles and poinsettia-spangled Ventura, about sixty miles apart.

It was between Thanksgiving and Christmas in 1972, the eighth year of the United States' involvement in the unpopular Vietnam War.

A short, rather stocky, balding electrical contractor came to Terry J. Moyer, then a high school history teacher and bishop of Santa Susana First Ward, Simi Valley California Stake.

The electrician began:

"Bishop, some years ago, I was in a bind financially. A bishop in another area provided me and my family with goods and cash."

The electrician handed Bishop Moyer a $100 greenback.

"Use it to help someone who needs it," the caller said.

A woman in the ward a day or two afterward called on Bishop Moyer. Her husband was in jail on a minor offense. She wanted him home with the family for Christmas. She had scrimped and scratched, she said. She had sold her guitar and her tape recorder. She needed $106 more for bail. The electrician's $100, with $6 from the bishop, was provided. The husband joined his family Christmas Eve.

But the happy story did not end there. Each year for several years between Thanksgiving and Christmas, the grateful electrician brought $100 to the bishop "to help someone out."

As Thanksgiving approaches, it is a golden time for family togetherness, turkey, cranberries and homemade ice cream.

Thanksgiving can glow even more if it becomes a time for giving special thanks—like that of a balding electrician in Simi Valley.

John K. Nicksich is a United Way officer who witnesses much quiet, action-filled gratitude. He tells of a young widow who was assisted two years ago by the Hospice program when her twenty-seven-year-old husband died of cancer. Hospice's volunteers and trained nurses help prepare people for the impending death of a loved one. Since then the grateful widow, Erna Simonson, as a Hospice volunteer, has been bringing solace to sorrowing strangers facing death.

Marcus Tullius Cicero, the great Roman orator and statesman, wrote: "Of all virtues, there is no quality I would rather have . . . than gratitude. For it is not only the greatest virtue, but even the mother of all the rest."[1]

Fulton Oursler, the American editor-author who penned *The Greatest Story Ever Told*, wrote about George C. Boldt, a Philadelphia hotel man. He gave up his own room to an elderly stranger and wife. Two years later Boldt was made manager of New York's famed Waldorf Astoria Hotel—by the stranger. His name: William Waldorf Astor.[2]

In a western city, some twenty-five years ago, the son of a struggling widow was counseled by his stake president to prepare for a career in real estate. More than twenty years later, the youth, now a successful developer, brought to the office of that tennis-playing stake president a beautiful bronze sculpture of a tennis player, with an engraved expression of thanks.

A BYU coed placed on her father's pillow a plate of carrot cookies she had made—with a note of gratitude for a fatherly favor, explaining that the cookies had been made with carrots from his home garden.

One of the powerful expressions of thanksgiving in the Bible was a mother-son offering:

Of Hannah and Samuel.

Childless Hannah prayed to the Lord for a son.

To her was born Samuel.

Thankfully, she told her God: "As long as he [Samuel] liveth he shall be lent to the Lord." (1 Samuel 1:28.)

Samuel became a mighty prophet, who anointed Saul and David as Israel's kings.

Much is spoken of the Good Samaritan, as indeed it should.

Much should also be spoken of the Grateful Samaritan: he who was the one of ten lepers Jesus healed who turned back. The Samaritan fell at his Master's feet "giving him thanks." (Luke 17:16.)

Thanksgiving: a wonderful time to be a "Grateful Samaritan."

Notes

1. *Pro Plancio*, Ch. 33, Sec. 80.

2. *Time* Oct. 10, 1949, p. 67.

39

Peace and a Child of Eight

Thirty-nine years ago, three months after the end of World War II, *Time* newsmagazine published this story:

"In the world's largest city last week, toward the middle of the 20th Century after Christ, five years after the Great Blitz, in the fifth month of the Atomic Age, an 8-year-old boy was asked what he wanted to be when he grew up. Said London's child:

" 'Alive.' "[1]

Today an eight-year-old child anywhere on this good earth could very well respond to the same question with the same answer.

The world's two superpowers continue to build their arsenals of nuclear weapons. They dwarf in destructive power the atomic bomb that exploded over Hiroshima in 1945, four months before that London lad responded: "Alive."

A few months ago the second-biennial conference On the Fate of the Earth was held in Washington, D.C.[2] On its eve, the Associated Press reported:

"Nineteen Nobel prize scientists and 178 leaders of environmental and arms reduction groups said Wednesday:

" 'Unless humanity changes its ways, mankind faces extinction either through a nuclear war or an environmental catastrophe.' "[3]

That is a sobering message.

One may not agree with all it says nor with all that was spoken at that conference.

But all thinking men and women would agree that more than ever peace must be pursued vigorously. Leaders of the two superpowers must strive harder to reduce nuclear armaments.

Where can a true and lasting peace be found for an eight-year-old—and for all mankind?

As Christmas approaches, probably millions of children will be asking for high-tech robotic action toys. Sales of this type of toys last year reached $325 million. "The craze has just begun," reports a respected newsletter.[4]

Robots and development of robotic machines are big news today. "After 190 years of counting the people, the Census Bureau has decided to determine the number of robots in the country," the Associated Press reports.[5]

There is certainly nothing particularly wrong about robotic toys for children.

But they will receive much, much more if they receive the precious, even priceless, gift of true peace.

"Peace does not dwell in outward things, but within the soul," wrote Francis de S. Fenelon, a French churchman and author (1651–1715).

A newspaper in South Korea, *The Yeungnam Observer*, this year published an article written by Rich Radford, previously a senior at George Washington University (Washington, D.C.) serving as a missionary for the Church in Korea.

Wrote Elder Radford: "Our Heavenly Father has provided rules for His children . . . lighthouses . . . Our destiny, our ability to move forward as nations and as a planet rests entirely on the resolve of each individual."

Peace, indeed, begins in the bosom of the individual—in observing the rules of the Prince of Peace.

Wrote Nephi following the death of his prophet-father Lehi: "Yea, why should I give way to temptations, that the evil one . . . destroy my peace." (2 Nephi 4:27.)

And in the great vision to President Joseph F. Smith is recorded: "But among the righteous there was peace." (D&C 138:22.)

An eight-year-old child today looks for peace in a day of robots and threat of nuclear war. He looks for life in the misty tomorrows ahead.

He can find peace. He can find life—an everlasting life of joy.

The way is simple: in realizing he is a child of God and in earnestly striving to live his Father's rules.

Surely the Lord was speaking to him when He said: "Learn of me, and listen to my words; walk in the meekness of my Spirit, and you shall have peace in me." (D&C 19:23.)

Notes

1. *Time,* Dec. 17, 1945, p. 27.
2. Sept. 19–23, 1984.
3. Sept. 19, 1984.
4. *John Naisbitt's Trend Letter,* Oct. 4, 1984.
5. Oct. 26, 1984.

40

Preparing
for Christmas

December is a wonderful time of the year, when thoughts turn to Christmas around the world.

Along Norway's fjords and towering waterfalls there are plans for making Christmas pudding with a single almond. (Some Norsemen say the one who gets the almond will be next married.)

In Mexico there are thoughts of poinsettia (Flower of the Holy Night) and piñatas.

Cookies shaped like people, animals, hearts, and stars soon will be made in Germany, to go on Christmas trees.

In England there will be plum pudding, and in Scotland, oat-meal cookies called bannock cakes.

Already in France, children are pondering about gifts going into shoes, placed in front of the fireplace on Christmas Eve.

Among Armenians in the Mideast, soon there will be talk of spinach. Many of them eat boiled spinach on Christmas Eve, believing the Virgin Mary ate spinach the night before Jesus was born.

Alice Thurston warmly describes Christmas preparation:

> Yet still in my heart and bright as an ember
> Is the memory sweet of quiet September.

Quiet September, when the lamp's amber core
Revealed Mother sewing, building her store:
Gifts for the lonely, gifts for the poor,
For her own brood and the child at the door.
Oh, always, always will I remember
The beginning of Christmas in quiet September.

Good people, like that mother in September, prepared for Christmas long before the Babe was born in a manger in Bethlehem.

Adam, some four thousand years before that holy night, taught his children of the coming of the Redeemer.

"And Eve, his wife, heard all these things and was glad." (Moses 5:11.)

As Adam and Eve affirmed the distant coming of the Lord and shared that truth with others, they found joy.

Enoch, son of Jared and father of Methuselah, spoke specifically of Jesus Christ as the author of salvation.

Moses and others, with sacrifices on the altar, prepared for the glory of the supreme sacrifice.

David wrote sublimely in his psalms of the Messiah who would come a thousand years later.

Centuries before the star shone over Bethlehem, a man whose flocks had covered the hills but who had lost his wealth and his ten children wrote gloriously of Jesus.

Declared Job: "For I know that my redeemer liveth, and that he shall stand at the latter day upon the earth:

"And though after my skin worms destroy this body, yet in my flesh shall I see God." (Job 19:25—26.)

Isaiah, the great prophet-statesman, penned musically of the Babe who would be born to a virgin—more than seven centuries before the nativity.

In the Western Hemisphere other good and happy people prepared centuries before the arrival of the Messiah.

Nephi foretold of the Sonship to a virgin. Alma named the area of His birth. Samuel the Lamanite told of His coming, and declared that those who followed Him "shall have everlasting life." (Helaman 14:8.)

Preparation for that first Christmas was joyous for two cousins: Elisabeth, mother of the Baptist, and Mary, mother of

Jesus. For three months they visited in Elisabeth's home in the hills of Judea, some hundred miles from Nazareth.

To Mary, Elisabeth said:

"Blessed art thou among women."

Responded Mary:

"My soul doth magnify the Lord." (Luke 1:42, 46.)

Preparing for Christmas indeed is a wonderful time. It is a joyous time for him or her who focuses on Him, as did Elisabeth and Mary and the prophets before.

It is a time of gladness if one's thoughts and preparations are for others. Remember how Jesus said: "Inasmuch as ye have done it unto one of the least of these my brethren, ye have done it unto me." (Matthew 25:40.)

41

Man Before the Man

He has probably had more influence on this year's Brigham Young University football team, the nation's only undefeated major college team, than any other man except LaVell Edwards, head coach.

He similarly has likely done more to mold BYU's football success that has resulted in nine consecutive Western Athletic Conference championships, except for Coach Edwards.

His powerful influence was there when the Cougars met Michigan University's Wolverines in the Holiday Bowl in a nationally televised game on Friday, Dec. 21, 1984, in San Diego, California.

He has been there at the games in Cougar Stadium, often wearing a blue "Y" jacket, with a blue and white baseball cap resting atop his bald head. His brown eyes smile and his wizened, lightly tanned face glows when BYU quarterback Robbie Bosco throws a touchdown pass.

He is eighty-five years old and still a farmer, raising his own peas, corn, squash, potatoes, and radishes in his plot near Utah Lake. He has served long as a school board chairman, as an Orem City councilman, as a bishop, and as a stake president.

Yet his education never went beyond the eighth grade. He is father of thirteen children, all but one (a daughter who died of cancer) are still living and active in the Church. He and Addie May Gurr Edwards have been married sixty-seven years.

He is Philo Taylor Edwards, father of Coach Edwards.

Asked, after BYU was unanimously ranked No. 1 by all the major college football polls, who had influenced his life more than any other, Coach Edwards unhesitatingly replied: "My father."

"I was born during the Great Depression, in 1930," Coach Edwards said. "Times were tough. I was the eighth of the thirteen children. There were really fourteen children because my parents raised from infancy a daughter of my father's sister, after she was taken by death. Our farmhouse was a low, light brick place with only one bath and two bedrooms. There were usually ten of us children at home at one time. The girls slept in one bedroom, my parents in the other. We boys slumbered in the basement, three of us in one bed.

"My father never lectured to us. He loved the restored gospel. He was not a great reader of the scriptures, but I never knew anyone who lived them better. He lived the same in our humble home as he did out as a Church or community leader.

"When our family would go on vacation, my father always made it a point to locate the local LDS meetinghouse—and we were in meetings on Sunday, the same as at home."

Coach Edwards continued:

"I watched the people who came to our Orem, Utah, home for advice from my father: the destitute and discouraged, BYU professors, businessmen, young men and women. My father listened. Quietly, he showed so much compassion."

LaVell Edwards, balding like his father, mused at his desk in his blue-carpeted room in the George Albert Smith Fieldhouse on the BYU campus. He wore a dark blue, V-necked sweater with a white shirt, opened at the neck. Behind him were several autographed and inscribed footballs. Here and there were small trophies and a carved stone cougar. On the oak paneled wall directly opposite him was a large oil painting of a rugged mountain.

"I like that painting—don't know the artist's name," he said.

The conversation turned again to his hero:

"My father would never pin me down or scold me. Sometimes I wished he would get mad at me when I erred a bit or pulled a prank. He would say to me:

" 'Son, I have confidence in you. I never worry about you.'

"Nothing impressed me more than my father's integrity. When he was stake president, the visiting General Authority at stake conference time would come to our home for Sunday dinner. Father would tell us kids to act the same when the General Authority was in our home as we always did—even if it meant eyeing the hoop on the side of the barn."

As if taking a page from his father's book, LaVell, who has also served as a bishop, once said: "The players know they can come in and talk to me anytime about personal problems or whatever is on their mind."

USA Today quoted Pittsburgh University's Coach Foge Fazio on LaVell Edwards:

"He is really a great coach as well as a great man."[1]

LaVell Edwards would respond modestly about his hero:

"My father inside home and out is a living scripture."

Notes

1. Nov. 20, 1984, p. 2C.

42

Towering
but Tender

It was a rented sixty-eight-acre farm with rocky soil almost midway in the length of Vermont, some twenty miles east of the Green Mountain ridge.

The family was poor. It was winter. The day was December 23. The year was 1805, the same year Napoleon Bonaparte, already emperor of France, was crowned King of Italy. Two years before, President Thomas Jefferson had purchased from Napoleon the entire Louisiana Territory—all or parts of fifteen states today— for a mere $15 million.

The boy born that December day in obscure Sharon, Vermont, was given the plainest of names: Joseph Smith.

In the next ten years, Joseph's struggling family lived in five different locations in New England. Then they moved to the wilderness of western New York.

Joseph worked hard with his hands. His education was meager. He never attended high school or college, yet his was a most remarkable life.

At fourteen as a plowboy he experienced one of the most wondrous theophanies of all time—a visitation of the Father and Son.

At twenty-four he gave to the world the first printed copies of the Book of Mormon, another testament of Jesus Christ. Since that time, approximately 25 million copies of the book have been printed. Today it appears in thirty-nine different languages.

Also at twenty-four he organized The Church of Jesus Christ of Latter-day Saints, whose members today number more than 5.5 million. The Church has been described as the fastest-growing major denomination in the United States. Yet the convert baptisms outside the U.S. today are approximately three times those within.

At thirty-one he launched missionary work outside North America. Today nearly 27,000 missionaries serve in 182 missions around the world.

At thirty-four he founded beautiful Nauvoo, which in several years became one of the largest cities in Illinois, with a chartered university and an impressive temple.

At thirty-six he organized in Nauvoo what today is called the Relief Society, one of America's first women's organizations and today one of the world's largest, with more than 1.8 million members.

At thirty-eight he was slain in a Carthage, Illinois jail by a mob with painted faces, leaving the Church with some 26,146 hounded members. Under Joseph Smith's protege-successor, Brigham Young, they completed one of the great exoduses in history—to America's Mountain West. There in a desert wilderness they established more than three hundred cities and towns. As a people today they are known for their high educational levels, superior work ethic and health, and with more than their share of achievers in a wide range of disciplines and pursuits.

History must acknowledge the greatness of Joseph Smith, with all his accomplishments and those of his followers. His stature grows with the years.

His achievements came because he was indeed a Prophet of God—the restoring instrument of the pure gospel of Jesus the Christ, and of His divine Church.

John Taylor, who was with the Prophet in Carthage Jail when he met his death and who later presided over the Church, wrote: "Joseph Smith, the Prophet and Seer of the Lord, has done more, save Jesus only, for the salvation of men in this world, than any other man that ever lived in it." (D&C 135:3.)

With all his towering greatness, with all his achievements and persecutions, Joseph Smith remained a warm, "down on the farm" human being.

One example:

Mrs. Margaret Burgess, who later resided in St. George, Utah, recalled how as a child she lived with her parents near Joseph Smith's home in Nauvoo.

Margaret's mother gave birth to twins about the same time the Prophet's wife Emma lost a child at birth.

The Prophet called at the neighbor's home and asked if he could borrow one of the twins for a day. He took the child home to comfort Emma, returning the child in the evening. This procedure was repeated for several weeks, until Emma felt better.

The Prophet discontinued calling for the twin, but he frequently came to see her.

Indeed Joseph Smith was a mighty man of God with a tender heart!

43

Vacant Chair on Christmas

He was father of six. The family's modest light-yellow brick bungalow stood on a wide hillside road on the outskirts of town.

He was heavyset, six-footish. His thin, brown hair had a touch of curl. His was a prominent nose, and he squinted with one of his hazel eyes. He managed a building supply business. He liked to tell Scottish jokes and balance hats, sticks, and chairs on his ruddy, dimpled chin.

He was bishop in a small, growing ward.

It was custom in his home to begin Christmas morning with a prayer and breakfast of hot Cream of Wheat mush (cereal today).

Then the children, three girls and three boys, would form a line. The heavy, wood sliding doors to the living room would be pushed back by Mother. The children, all properly dressed, filed into the living room, festooned with twisted strands of red and green crepe paper.

Each child moved quickly to his or her loaded white stocking hanging before the fireplace. Awaiting them, too, were a few other presents on or around oak, leather-seated chairs: Mother-made aprons, pinafores, nightgowns, and doll clothes for the girls; a box of wood blocks, a sweater or cap for the boys.

"Don't make too much noise, kids," Mother smiled. "Don't bother Dad."

For years before he was bishop, while he so served, and for years afterward, Dad was never there for the first excitement of Christmas morning.

He remained in bed.

His chair was always empty.

He was adored by his wife and children. Yet little, if anything, was said of his absence on Christmas morning—year after year after year.

But one particular yule something was said about him.

The two younger, blond daughters the night before had watched from their bedroom window when his car arrived late in the family driveway.

Roped to the car were two small pink dressers. The daughters, in nightgowns, were excited. A pink dresser for each!

Next morning, when the family marched into the living room, there was only one pink dresser beside the vacant chair. There was the sweet aroma of pine wood and fresh paint. The dresser had been custom made by a cabinetmaker near Father's business.

Mother drew the two sisters to her side. Almost tearfully she explained:

"There were two pink dressers, one for each of you. But last night your father thought of a widow's family. She had two daughters, too. Your father decided to take one of the pink dressers to her home. This one here this morning is for you to share."

They shared it in their bedroom for some fifteen years. They shared it after they were married. Then their daughters shared it. Granddaughters now share it.

This year one of the sisters recalled with a brother some of the many needy people they suspected their father helped on those many Christmas Eves:

An elderly woman living with a mature retarded daughter in a wood shack beside an oak grove through the fields from their home.

Struggling Scottish folk—friends of their father's since his missionary days in the Highlands. Others.

In that yellow brick bungalow on Christmas morns, a loyal, loving mother carried on with the children.

She knew why the oak chair was vacant. She had tenderly encouraged her companion to remain in bed and rest, after being out a good part of the night bringing a brighter yule to the needy.

The children knew. That is one of the reasons they loved and admired Father and Mother so much.

A pink dresser today reminds them of the true meaning of that vacant chair—as expressed by the supreme center of all Christmas activities, Jesus the Christ:

"Take heed that ye do not your alms before men, to be seen of them. . . .

"That thine alms may be in secret." (Matthew 6:1, 4.)

44

Two Men at Geneva

The eyes and ears of a hopeful world will focus a week after New Year's, 1985, on a charming city at the tip of a long Swiss lake: Geneva.

Geneva will bring together two formidable diplomats, representing the world's two superpowers. The two men will confer on nuclear arms. Hopefully curbs will eventually result.

Representing Russia will be its foreign minister of twenty-seven years. Andrei Andreyevich Gromyko, seventy-five years old, with abundant, slate-gray hair and a dour, dark-eyed face.

He is a son of well-to-do peasants. He toiled as a youth on the family farm near Minsk.

Gromyko reads much. Favorite authors include Byron, Hugo, Goethe, and Shakespeare. Through the years he has enjoyed stamp collecting, volleyball, boar hunting, and playing chess with his wife, Lidiya. They have two children.

He has been in Russia's foreign service for forty-five years. He has dealt with nine U.S. presidents. He is "not only custodian of Moscow's foreign policy, but probably its chief architect," according to *Time*.[1]

The U.S. representative at Geneva will be stocky, blue-eyed, soft-spoken George Pratt Shultz, sixty-four, with thinning, graying sandy hair.

Only son of a New York Ph.D. in history, he majored in ecomonics at Princeton, where he played basketball and was a football halfback.

Shultz has been an educator much of his adult life. As a Marine in World War II he met and later married a nurse, Helena O'Brien. They have five adult children.

He first served in the U.S. government as fiscal adviser to President Dwight D. Eisenhower, and has since served as Labor Secretary, Treasury Secretary, and Budget Director.

Prior to being named Secretary of State in 1982 by President Ronald Reagan, he was president of Bechtel, a giant construction company based in San Francisco.

Shultz has been described as a "team player" and "a man of uncommon integrity."

The stakes and hopes are high for the Geneva meeting of Shultz and Gromyko.

Both these able men—one a Christian (Episcopalian); the other a Communist—could draw some helpful lessons for their talks from an eminently successful ancient statesman.

He lived in tumultuous times—of shifting ideologies and tumbling empires. He began his career about six centuries before the birth of Christ. He was a king's ruler under several conquerors. The great Nebuchadnezzar named him governor over all Babylon's wise men. Belshazzar, king of the Chaldeans, designated him third ruler of the empire.

Darius, the Median, took over the kingdom after Belshazzar was slain. Darius named him first among his counselors.

His name?

Daniel.

Daniel was a master negotiator. Nebuchadnezzar had a disturbing dream. But he forgot it. He asked his wise men to tell him the dream and interpret it. If they delivered: rich rewards, great honor. If they failed: death.

Daniel was among those who might be slain. To the king's captain, ordered to execute the order, Daniel asked for time.

"Why is the decree so hasty from the king?" he inquired. (Daniel 2:15.)

Then Daniel asked the king for time. He got it. He prayed for an answer. He got it. The king made Daniel a ruler.

Other strengths of Daniel:

He was mindful of the people, the common people. To Nebuchadnezzar, teetotaling Daniel said boldly: "Break off thy sins by righteousness, and thine iniquities by shewing mercy to the poor." (Daniel 4:27.)

Daniel seemed to carry with him a spirit of love for others. Darius, it is recorded, placed Daniel foremost among the king's rulers "because an excellent spirit was in him." (Daniel 6:3.)

Humility was a Daniel strength.

To Belshazzar, who held out rich rewards to Daniel, the Israelite said: "Let thy gifts be to thyself, and give thy rewards to another." (Daniel 5:17.)

Daniel repeatedly sought his God for skills beyond his own. Of the Lord, Daniel wrote: "He giveth wisdom to the wise." (Daniel 2:21.)

Daniel had a grateful heart. His first thankfulness was to his Maker.

"He kneeled upon his knees three times a day, and prayed, and gave thanks before his God, as he did aforetime." (Daniel 6:10.)

A watchful waiting world hopefully will pray fervently for the two diplomats in their momentous meetings.

May some of us pray, too, that the spirit of Daniel will be there also in that conference room in Geneva.

Notes

1. *Time*, June 25, 1984, p. 24.

45

Book of Light

The little book is 150 years old.

It measures approximately five by seven inches and is roughly three-quarters of an inch thick. The worn, dark brown leather cover is peeled off at the corners, revealing the cardboard underlayer.

The old book's two covers are laced together by faded, narrow, white cords or string. The pages are yellow, a darker hue around the edges. Some pages are slightly dog-eared.

The heavy, black type is clear.

The first line on the title page: Doctrine and Covenants.

The bottom line on the page is the year of publication: 1835.

This is one of the original copies of the first edition of one of the four standard scriptures of the Church: the Doctrine and Covenants.

This book is unique among the four. The other three are largely translations from ancient writings. These three are the Bible, Book of Mormon, and Pearl of Great Price.

The Doctrine and Covenants contains modern revelations and official declarations. The first of the published revelations was received in 1823 by the Prophet Joseph Smith, then seventeen years old, at the farming hamlet of Manchester in western New York. The section is part of a message from the angel Moroni. The last declaration in the book is signed by the First Presidency of Spencer W. Kimball, N. Eldon Tanner, and Marion G. Romney, and dated June 8, 1978. This declaration extends the opportunity to hold the priesthood to all worthy male members "without regard for race or color." (Official Declaration—2.)

At a general assembly of the Church in Kirtland, Ohio (near Cleveland) on August 17, 1835, the Doctrine and Covenants was accepted. At the assembly was read a testimony of the Twelve Apostles affirming "that these commandments were given by inspiration of God."

This message of the Twelve was dated February 17, 1835— just three days after the original Twelve of this dispensation were organized in a schoolhouse in Kirtland.

This remarkable scripture is indeed a book of light.

Repeatedly the Doctrine and Covenants refers to Jesus the Christ as "light of the world" or "light that shineth in darkness."

In the fiftieth section the Lord declares:

"That which is of God is light; and he that receiveth light, and continueth in God, receiveth more light; and that light groweth brighter and brighter until the perfect day." (D&C 50:24.)

Revelations between 1823 and 1978? Are these messages of light for real?

That question the world, if interested enough, asks.

Twelve Apostles 150 years ago affirmed that revelations in the Doctrine and Covenants were genuine. How genuine were those twelve men?

Let us look quickly at several of them.

One was Brigham Young. Historians and respected leaders and observers have praised him for his character and achievements.

Cecil B. DeMille, the great motion picture magnate, said of him:

"Moses and Brigham Young were both strong leaders of a strong people. . . . They were lawgivers and they were educators."[1]

Heber C. Kimball, another one of those testifying Apostles who became a powerful figure in the founding of the Mountain West, was described by Mark Twain: ". . . that shrewd Connecticut Yankee, Heber C. Kimball, a saint of high degree and a mighty man of commerce."[2]

Orson Pratt, also one of the original Twelve, was saluted in a London volume by Jules Remy and Julius Benchley in 1861. "Orson Pratt, apostle, philosopher, theologian, a man of considerable learning, more especially in mathematics and astronomy; a pure and upright-minded man."[3]

Illinois Governor, Thomas Carlin, in 1840, after making the acquaintance of Orson Hyde and hearing him preach, recommended him as a man of "Christian-like deportments" and "entitled to the respect and kind treatment of all."[4]

Five years before, Orson Hyde was one of the Twelve affirming the divinity of the Doctrine and Covenants.

The volume has stood the test of time. It today continues to be a "book of light"—lifting lives around the world with its lofty messages from the Master, revealed through modern prophets.

Notes

1. Commencement address, Brigham Young University, May 31, 1957.

2. Twain, Mark, *Roughing It*, (Hartford, Connecticut, American Publishing, 1872), p. 112.

3. *A Journey to Great Salt Lake City*, vol. 2, pp. 186–7.

4. Letter dated April 30, 1840, contained in "An Historical Study of the Life of Orson Hyde," by Marvin S. Hill, Master's Thesis, Brigham Young University, 1955, p. 114.

46

Mighty Men of Music

Music, since the beginning of earthly time, has lifted lives nearer to the Lord.

In 1985, the world celebrated the three hundredth year of the births of two mighty masters of majestic music: Johann Sebastian Bach and George Frederic Handel.

Bach and Handel have stirringly and abundantly enriched our Latter-day Saint music. And what church people today are better known for their song?

Bach and Handel were born in 1685.

Bach's German father taught him to play the violin as a tot. An orphan at nine, he went to live with an older brother, who taught him to play keyboard instruments.

Bach's brother became envious of his musical skills, and the boy secretly borrowed a collection of manuscript compositions of the day. By the light of the moon through six months he laboriously copied the music.

At fifteen Bach was named a church chorister; at nineteen, organist.

When twenty-two, he married a cousin, Maria Barbara Bach. They had seven children. She died when he was thirty-five. The following year he married Anna Magdalena Wilcken, a professional singer. They had thirteen children.

A devout Lutheran, he had a family life as happy as an ensemble of joyous strings. Anna wrote out the parts of many of his religious cantatas.

He was recognized in his day as a gifted organist, and sacred music for choruses and orchestras poured from his pen like a mighty stream from heaven. Bach's complete works today fill about sixty volumes, yet only nine or ten were published while he lived.

It was seventy years after Bach's death that a brilliant German musician, only fourteen years old, found an almost forgotten manuscript at his teacher's home. It was Bach's *St. Matthew Passion.*

The young musician, six years later, gave a public performance of the complex work, calling for two sets of choruses and orchestras. It was a resounding success.

The young musician was Felix Mendelssohn, a Christian Jew.

That performance started a growing world acclaim of the genius of Johann Sebastian Bach, almost forgotten since his death.

Today, on its CBS network broadcast, the Mormon Tabernacle Choir frequently presents music from Bach. So do the great symphonies around the world.

"He knew his kinship with divinity so well," wrote Elbert Hubbard of Bach.[1]

Handel's career was much different from Bach's. In Handel's lifetime he was esteemed by royalty in Europe and Britain—both as a mighty organist and as a composer. The music world acclaimed him. Bach was buried in an obscure German grave. Handel was buried among the great in Westminster Abbey, with a magnificent monument.

Handel never married.

He was born in Halle, now in the German Democratic Republic, known today for its production of salt and machinery.

His father was a barber who later became a surgeon.

At twelve, Handel became assistant organist at the Cathedral of Halle. In that year he composed two sonatas. At nineteen he wrote two operas. When he was twenty-two he wrote his first

Italian opera, and at twenty-five produced two oratorios in Rome.

The day after his twenty-sixth birthday he produced his opera *Rinaldo* in London.

He became a British citizen. In his fifty's he turned from composing opera to oratorios. At fifty-seven in Dublin he produced his *Messiah*, the masterpiece for which he is most remembered. He wrote other impressive oratorios, usually on biblical subjects.

At the first London performance of *Messiah*, when the "Hallelujah Chorus" thundered out, "the entire audience rose like one man."

In his later years, Handel became totally blind. In darkness, he presided at the organ for a performance of his *Messiah* when he was seventy-four. Eight days later, on the Saturday between Good Friday and Easter, he died.

We shall hear much of Bach and Handel in music halls and church services. The world no doubt will be stirred and strengthened by the surging swells of their wondrous works for generations to come.

For which we can shout "Bravo!" And thank the Lord for giving us these two mighty men of music.

———————————

Notes

1. Hubbard, Elbert, *Little Journeys to the Homes of Great Musicians,* (East Aurora, Erie County, New York, Roycrofters, 1901), p. 136.

47

Giving with Your Ears

During World War II, John N. Monroe, a tall Texan, developed a keen listening ear for Indonesian and Malaysian dialects.

He interpreted them for the United States armed forces.

Now, for motorists who know little about mechanics, he interprets car noises. He has recorded them on tapes to assist people in detecting car trouble.

One set of his tapes offers 467 different "car trouble" sounds.

His company operates out of Waco, Texas, where he once taught geology at Baylor University.

He aims to teach Americans now what he calls "the language of cars."

Cheers for Mr. Monroe, for developing superb listenership, for creatively helping people with car trouble!

But most all of us need to learn how to better listen to *people.*

"The ear is the road to the heart," wrote Voltaire,[1] the great eighteenth century French author and philosopher.

Job said it even better:

"When the ear heard me, then it blessed me." (Job 29:11.)

A few Sundays ago a white-haired patriarch[2] answered the door to his white, shingle-sided gable home near a grove of oaks in the Mountain West.

The caller was a prominent member of the patriarch's stake. The visitor came for counsel. Business reverses had begun to affect his health.

"He remained for over three hours," the patriarch said, not divulging the caller's identity.

"About all I did was listen," the patriarch continued. "I nodded now and again to let my friend know I was alert. But mostly I just listened."

Listening is one of the noblest, most helpful ways of giving of ourselves—to the blessings of others, as Job wrote.

Jane N. Daynes, San Diego California East Stake Primary president, tells of Robby, age eleven. A good athlete, he had a bad experience both with the coach and team in a summer baseball league.

The next year, he refused to play baseball. His parents were upset, disappointed.

But Robby's mother took time to listen. She sat down with him, with an interested ear. She learned Robby's real problem: he was afraid of being hit by the ball. His father worked with him and his fear. Robby did play ball on the team—and enjoyed it.

In Tulsa, Oklahoma, a ward Primary was preparing for a Mother's Day program. During the practice, a Blazer boy (eleven years old) became angry and left the room. A Primary leader[3] found the tall, brown-haired boy, invited him to return. He refused, said he did not like Primary, his Boy Scout adviser, or the bishop.

The Primary leader sat down with the boy. Then she listened. She discovered that the lad's mother had just left his father and children, and moved away. The Mother's Day program was apparently too much for the boy to handle.

The Primary leader listened more. She found the lad loved to play the violin. She said she would ask the ward Primary president to let him perform for Sharing Time.

Today the boy is an active deacon.

Good listening can turn problems and lives around.

President Harold B. Lee told of an experience of one of his daughters with her firstborn son:

It was a warm summer night, and Mother was trying to finish canning some apricots.

As she worked frantically, her two little sons, one aged four and the other three, came pajama-clad into the kitchen. They were ready for her to hear them say their prayers.

Not wishing to be interrupted, she said:

"Now boys, why don't you just run in and say your prayers alone tonight and Mother will keep working with these apricots."

David, the older of the two tots, paused in front of his mother, then said:

"But Mommy, which is more important, prayers or apricots?"[4]

Peter, the first Apostle, has reminded us that in listening, the Lord is the Exemplar. Wrote Peter: "For the eyes of the Lord are over the righteous, and his ears are open unto their prayers." (1 Peter 3:12.)

Notes

1. *Reponse au Roi de Prusse.*
2. O. Layton Alldredge.
3. Lisa S. South, Tulsa Oklahoma Stake Primary president.
4. *Strengthening the Home,* a brochure, 1973, pp. 6–7.

48

Learning to Be King

It has a "world-wide reputation for producing leaders," reports *The Wall Street Journal*[1] about Sandhurst.

Sandhurst is the popular name of Great Britain's Royal Military Academy, situated in Surrey on picturesque grounds with a lake, some thirty miles southwest of London.

Under Sandhurst's strict discipline, young Winston Churchill began to flower as a leader after being the "lowest boy in the lowest class" at Harrow, a leading English secondary school.

Founded in 1799, Sandhurst also trained Field Marshall Sir Bernard Montgomery, Britain's heroic World War II commander. The sultan of Oman was a student at Sandhurst. So was Jordan's King Hussein, who said of Sandhurst, "The finest place for a man to learn to be a king."

Of Sandhurst's 775 cadets today, 54 are foreigners.

Sandhurst's textbook on leadership displays these lines from the great Greek playwright, Euripides, who was a close friend of Socrates:

"Ten good soldiers wisely led
Will beat a hundred without a head."

The world seeks able leaders today—in business, government, community affairs, religion, culture, and, most important of all, in the home.

There are reasons Latter-day Saints should produce more than their share of both good and effective leaders. One big reason is our greater store of scriptures describing the ways of noble, God-fearing leaders.

In its lengthy report on Sandhurst, *The Wall Street Journal* tells of some of Sandhurst's teaching tenets for leadership. For each of these there are vivid examples in lives from Latter-day Saint scriptures.

Reports the *Journal* on Sandhurst:

"We must be very careful to ensure that when we speak, our meaning is crystal clear."

A mighty prophet-ruler was King Benjamin, "a holy man, and he did reign over his people in righteousness." (Words of Mormon 1:17.) One of his strengths: communicating effectively with clarity. To address his people he built a tall tower. When his voice from the tower did not reach all of the vast assembled throng, he caused that his talk be written and distributed among those who could not hear.

King Benjamin to his people spoke "plainly . . . that ye might understand." (Mosiah 2:40.)

Of Sandhurst, the *Journal* says, it counsels its cadets as officers "to . . . remember that strict discipline helps men to face the unknown terrors of war."

King Benjamin taught discipline, concluding his tower talk: "Watch yourselves, and your thoughts, and your words, and your deeds, and observe the commandments of God." (Mosiah 4:30.)

Modern scriptures and other accounts tell of the superior leadership of Joseph Smith. On discipline and love, the Lord spoke to him: "Reproving betimes with sharpness, when moved upon by the Holy Ghost; and then showing forth afterwards an increase of love toward him whom thou hast reproved, lest he esteem thee to be his enemy." (D&C 121:43.)

Sandhurst, the *Journal* says, teaches: "The emphasis is on quick and independent thought," particularly in crisis situations.

The Book of Esther in the Bible records the courageous, quick, and independent action of a queenly woman. She, Esther, said of her bold plan to persuade the king: "And if I perish, I perish." (Esther 4:16.)

Read of the resourcefulness and courage of persecuted Paul, of Noah building the ark, and of Abinadi the prophet speaking boldly before a wicked king. And where can one find a better example of creative, courageous action than that of the youth David, armed only with a slingshot and pebbles, confronting towering Goliath, armed for war.

The *Journal* reports: "An officer, Sandhurst teaches, rarely shouts; that's for sergeants. An officer orders in a firm, steady tone. He isn't sarcastic."

One of the great leaders of the Old Testament was Joseph, who was sold into Egypt. As you read the account of his rise to the Pharaoh's ruler of Egypt, there is no hint of shouting in all Joseph's deep trials and glorious triumphs. But Genesis does record the Pharaoh's measure of Joseph: "There is none so discreet and wise as thou art." (Genesis 41:39.)

At Sandhurst, cadets are told: "Use 'we' instead of 'you' in addressing the troops; it fosters team spirit."

The [*Concordance of the Book of Mormon*] lists the use of the word "we" hundreds of times—by Nephi, Mosiah, Alma, and other prophets.

Sandhurst is an esteemed training ground for leadership. But the supreme textbook on the subject is holy writ, including the account of the earthly mission of the greatest of all leaders: Jesus the Christ, King of Kings.

Notes

1. Dec. 24, 1984, p. 1.

49

Special Witnesses

Ohio in 1835 was growing like a gourd. Settlements were mushrooming amid the vast forests that only three decades before were dotted mainly by Indian villages.

Kirtland was a booming Ohio town, some six miles inland from Lake Erie and twenty miles northeast of Cleveland. In five years Kirtland's population had doubled to 2,040, most of them farm folk from New England and New York. Roughly half of Kirtland's people in 1835 were Latter-day Saints.

Kirtland had its brickyard, clothing and shoe factory, carriage shop, printing office, gristmill, and steam sawmill.

On a Kirtland eminence, a sandstone-walled temple was rising, with thick walnut floors and oak beams.

On Saturday, February 14, 1835, the Prophet Joseph Smith called a special meeting of the Church in the schoolhouse "next to the rising temple."[1] Many of the attenders had the year before marched with Zion's Camp on the long, hazardous trek to Missouri.

The Prophet spoke and there were hymns and prayers. Then the meeting was adjourned for one hour. When the congregation reconvened, the Quorum of the Twelve was organized for the first time in this dispensation. The First Presidency[2] laid their hands on the Three Witnesses[3] and blessed them. Then the names of the Twelve, selected by the Witnesses, were read in this order:

1. Lyman E. Johnson
2. Brigham Young
3. Heber C. Kimball
4. Orson Hyde
5. David W. Patten
6. Luke S. Johnson
7. William E. McLellin
8. John F. Boynton
9. Orson Pratt
10. William Smith
11. Thomas B. Marsh
12. Parley P. Pratt

Later, the order of the original Twelve was rearranged according to age. This order placed Thomas B. Marsh as senior Apostle. In 1835 he was thirty-six years old, six years older than Joseph Smith and two years older than Brigham Young, who was third in the rearranged order, behind Elders Marsh and Patten.

The original Twelve were called from various occupations. Thomas B. Marsh was a farmer who had worked for some time in a hotel and who later became a frontier physician. Brigham Young was a carpenter, painter, and glazier. Heber C. Kimball for years had been in the pottery business. Orson Pratt was a farmer-scholar—an adept student of mathematics, grammar, and other subjects.

These were generally bright, rugged frontiersmen—worthy counterparts of the Twelve chosen by the Savior Himself in Palestine.

In former days, the Apostles forsook their occupations to serve as special witnesses of the Christ. So do they today.

Shortly after the Twelve were called in 1835, the Lord explained that, as in ancient days, they were "special witnesses of the name of Christ in all the world." (D&C 107:23.)

At least ninety-four men have been ordained Apostles in this dispensation. Most have remained valiant special witnesses. A few have become disaffected, and of these some have returned to the Church.

There have been some mighty men of God serving as modern members of the Twelve. Youngest ever ordained an Apostle was George A. (for Albert) Smith, big of body and keen of mind, called at twenty-one in 1839 in Missouri. He later served in the

First Presidency, was a powerful colonizer, able writer and speaker, educator, and statesman.

Oldest named an Apostle was kindly, genteel George Q. (for Quayle) Morris, chief executive of a successful stone and tile business. He was ordained an Apostle at eighty in 1954.

There have been distinguished men of science and learning such as Orson Pratt, James E. Talmage, John A. Widtsoe, and Joseph F. Merrill. There have been eminent statesmen such as George Q. (for Quayle) Cannon, who served in the U.S. Congress; Reed Smoot, for many years a U.S. Senate leader; and J. Reuben Clark, an Under Secretary of State and U.S. Ambassador to Mexico. Eloquent orators like Melvin J. Ballard, Matthew Cowley, and Hugh B. Brown have been Apostles. And there have been mighty missionaries, including Parley P. Pratt, Wilford Woodruff, and LeGrand Richards.

But, most of all, members of the Twelve have been special witnesses of the living Christ.

As we observe the 150th anniversary of the organization of the modern Council of the Twelve, it is well to contemplate the words of Jesus to His Apostles after they had supped together and He had washed their feet:

"Verily, verily, I say unto you, He that receiveth whomsoever I send receiveth me; and he that receiveth me receiveth him that sent me." (John 13:20.)

The Twelve are sent of Him. It is for us to receive them and heed their words as His chosen witnesses.

Notes

1. Backman, Milton V., Jr., *The Heavens Resound* (Salt Lake City, Utah, Deseret Book Company, 1983), p. 248.

2. The First Presidency in 1835 was comprised of Joseph Smith, Jr., President; Sidney Rigdon, First Counselor; and Frederick G. Williams, Second Counselor.   •

3. Oliver Cowdery, David Whitmer, and Martin Harris.

50

Molders of Men

Charles Mont Mahoney looks and acts like a frontiersman.

His crinkly, gray-brown hair crowns a leathery tan face with touches of pink at the cheeks. His far-seeing eyes are light blue. His six-feet three-inch height and two-hundred-pound weight have remained the same for some forty years. Heavy, thick-soled leather boots appear to cover his size thirteen feet more comfortably than oxfords or sneakers. A hammer or hatchet fits his calloused hands more naturally than a pen or pencil.

At sixty-two Mont Mahoney presides over a construction company that built the temples in Tonga and Samoa. Now his company is partner in constructing the Chicago Temple.

Mont and his bright, sturdy, blond wife, Ruth, reside in a low, yellow-orange brick and stone home on a brush-shawled, rocky mountainside where deer often bound. A twenty-five-foot flagpole, usually flying Old Glory, rises from the spacious front lawn.

They have five children.

Mont Mahoney for thirty years has been a Boy Scout leader, first as an administrator, then for eleven years as Scoutmaster.

For more than three years now he has been team coach with the Varsity Scouts (fourteen and fifteen years old).

Soon, Mont will lead about eight of his Scouts by snowmobile or three-wheeler into the high mountains for an overnight campout. They will sleep in oval caves they will carve out of the deep snows.

Mont has taken his Scouts down the eight-mile trail to the oasis-like bottom of Arizona's Grand Canyon. They have studied bald eagles in the sage-covered Oquirrh Mountains in northern Utah. Recently he honored one of his Scouts by baking for him a chocolate birthday cake, with decorated frosting, at 10,500 feet in Wyoming's towering Wind River Mountains—with a "reflector oven": a sheet of aluminum beside an open fire.

Of the some 150 Boy Scouts who have been led on these and other campouts by Mont Mahoney, approximately half have become Eagles, 90 percent have fulfilled Church missions, 80 percent have been married in the temple.

"You can get closer to boys around a campfire," declares Mont. "And there they seem to get closer to the Lord."

He can be tough on a whiner in camp.

Under Mont, to become an Eagle, boys must do more than earn the required merit badges. They must prove they are trustworthy and practice good citizenship at school.

Every trip begins with a prayer before departure, and there are supplications around the campfire, where Mont also bears his gospel testimony. He stresses that Scouting supports the priesthood.

One of his former scouts, Carl Empey, son of an FBI agent, wrote Mont from America's Southwest, where Carl was serving a mission among the Navajos: "I just want to thank you, Mont, for the care and love you gave me. . . . I use a lot of what I learned in Boy Scouts here on the reservation."

C. Mont Mahoney is one of 92,000 U.S. Latter-day Saint Scouters and 274,000 LDS Scouts in the nation who join others across America in commemorating Scouting's seventy-fifth anniversary in the U.S.

The percentage of the nation's youth (aged eight through eighteen) enrolled in Scouting has climbed from 15 percent in

1980 to 16 percent in 1983. Among U.S. Latter-day Saints, the percentage rise has been from 74 to 82 percent.

Among Mont Mahoney's treasures is a statuette of Lord Baden-Powell (Robert Stephenson Smyth Baden-Powell), founder of Scouting in 1907, in England.

In 1934, a Latter-day Saint youth visiting the office of Baden-Powell, Chief Scout of the World, on London's Buckingham Palace Road, made a discovery:

Hanging on the Chief's office wall was a color picture of a statue on Salt Lake City's Temple Square, inscribed, "Sea Gull Monument. Erected in Grateful Remembrance of the Mercy of God to the Mormon Pioneers."

Forty-nine years ago, Thomas J. Keane, New York City, director of Senior Scouting in America, declared:

"Worldwide Boy Scout activities attain their highest degree of excellence in Utah."[1]

The same no doubt could be said of U.S. Latter-day Saints today, when worldwide there are more than 16 million Boy Scouts and their leaders in 150 countries.

It could be said because of thousands of caring Latter-day Saint Scout leaders like tough, tender Charles Mont Mahoney — from Montevideo to Hong Kong and from Samoa to Switzerland.

Notes

1. *Millennial Star,* London, England, June 4, 1936, p. 363.

51

It Adds Power
to Prayer

It was March 1978 in Goteberg, Sweden's second largest city and Scandinavia's top ship-building center.

A blond, wiry Swede, Bjorn Borg, was king of the world's tennis. Four months before, a stake had been organized in Goteberg—Sweden's second.

A tall, trim, handsome, and black-haired missionary stumbled along a Goteberg Street. His name: Warren Jeff Hansen, 20 years old.

Before his mission Jeff had been his high school class president. He had loved both scuba and sky diving, and strumming a banjo.

On that March day in 1978, a mission leader noticed Jeff's halting walk.

A visit to a physician brought the numbing news: Jeff had multiple sclerosis.

A surgeon friend of Jeff's father hurriedly enplaned to Sweden, brought Jeff home.

His condition worsened.

Jeff's bishop announced a special weekday of fast for the returned missionary. At the end of the fast, in the evening, there would be a prayer meeting at the meetinghouse.

Old men and women responded. So did younger adults and small children.

The chapel was filled that evening. There were several short talks. "We need to be positive about Jeff's situation—not fearful," said a white-haired ward member, Elder Mark E. Petersen of the Council of the Twelve. "The Lord will bless him." A soul-lifting prayer was spoken. The service lasted some thirty minutes.

The proceedings were recorded and later played to Jeff on his sickbed.

That was seven years ago. Today, in 1985, Jeff is legally blind. At Christmastime he was in the hospital, in a coma for two days with an infection. He now gets around in a wheelchair.

But Jeff is happily married—to lovely brunette, JoAnn Crane, a convert with a law degree. They have two beautiful children: a son, three, and a daughter, six months.

JoAnn, who met Jeff three years after that special fast, spends hours reading to him. They attend church meetings faithfully in their student ward. Each month he does his home teaching.

Great are the blessings that come through prayerful fasting.

Especially is this so when a family, neighbors, a ward, a stake, many stakes, or the entire Church fasts on a special day or for a special purpose.

This was true with Jeff Hansen's ward. It was true on Sunday, January 27, 1985, when members of all stakes in the United States and Canada joined, at the request of the First Presidency, in fasting, praying, and contributing. The funds assisted the starving Ethiopians and others.

Anciently, beautiful Esther, Jewish queen of Persia, called all the Jews in Shushan, Persia's capital, to fast for three days and nights. The fast, in which Esther joined, was for her efforts in appealing to the king to spare the lives of the Jews. A royal decree had called for their destruction.

Courageous Queen Esther petitioned the king. Her people were spared. (See Esther 4–7.)

Alma "fasted and prayed many days" to know the things of God. (See Alma 5:46.)

"Fasting is a medicine," spoke golden-tongued Saint John Chrysostom, an early Christian born in Antioch.

Fasting can be much more. It can unify with spiritual ties. It can build humility and encourage giving. It adds power to prayer and sweetens sacrifice. It deepens and lengthens joy.

All these things fasting has done. It can do them today, starting with you.

52

Puff or Snuff, It's Tough

They called him "Alfalfa." He was just sixteen, with unkempt, dark brown hair. He was tall and lean, but heavy enough to play tackle on the high school football team. With his carpenter father, he liked to whip a fly over the streams and hunt pheasants and ducks near his home in Ontario, an Oregon farm town near the Idaho border.

He had begun to date. He wanted people to think him older than he was. He started smoking cigarettes.

Some twenty years later he was a family man and supervisor with a large electric appliance manufacturer. His name is James Robert Nelson, but most everyone calls him "Jim."

Jim was now smoking four packs a day—and night. At intervals of about two hours he would awaken from his sleep, smoke a cigarette, then return to his sleep.

Jim took a physical examination including a chest X ray. It showed spots on one of his lungs. He was scared. He quit smoking, fast.

About six years later, through the efforts of stake missionaries, he joined the Church.

Millions of Americans, like Jim Nelson, have kicked the cigarette habit because of health concerns. In three years, beginning in 1980, the percentage of U.S. adults smoking declined from 37 to 29 percent.

U.S. Surgeon General C. Everett Koop has appealed to all major health organizations to help "make non-smoking the national norm."

The American Lung Association aims for a smoke-free generation by the year 2000.

Dr. Kenneth Warner, University of Michigan professor who has made extensive studies on the economics of smoking, says the cost of cigarette smoking to every American (whether smoker or not) is approximately $140 each year.

Dr. Warner says tobacco is implicated in 80 to 90 percent of U.S. lung cancers, 30 percent of all cancer deaths, 30 percent of heart disease, and 80 to 90 percent of chronic obstructive pulmonary disease.[1]

In Jim Nelson's native Oregon a citizen's task force proposes a new state cigarette tax of eighty-eight cents a pack — "That's what the average pack of cigarettes sold in Oregon costs in health care expenditures," the committee explains.

Expanding, Dallas-based Muse Airlines bars smoking on all its flights.

MSI Insurance Co., Minneapolis, with seven hundred employees, now forbids smoking in all its offices.[2]

Surveys show, reports the American Cancer Society, that 85 percent of cigarette smokers would like to quit.[3]

Blond Gerrie D. Thompson, twenty-eight, a health educator and ex-smoker, now conducts stop-smoking clinics for the Society. She reports 50 to 90 percent of her enrollees kick the habit. One was a fourteen-year-old boy who had been smoking for five years.

It was 152 years ago, at a time when Andrew (Old Hickory) Jackson was president of the United States and when both smoking and chewing tobacco were popular, that the Prophet Joseph Smith at Kirtland, Ohio, received the revelation known as the Word of Wisdom. It declared: "And again, tobacco is not for the body . . . and is not good for man." (D&C 89:8.)

While praiseworthy gains have been made toward a smoke-less society, tobacco marketers continue to push. Next month, R.J. Reynolds will begin test-marketing "the last word in smoking chic": designer cigarettes. They feature the logo of France's Yves Saint Laurent (YSL) and aim at young women in their twenty's and thirty's.[4]

Today use of snuff and chewing tobacco is one of the nation's fastest-growing habits, particularly among youth. During 1971–81, chewing tobacco increased by 50 percent.

But medical research confirms that tobacco in any form "is not for the body." Dr. Arden G. Christen, chairman of the department of preventive dentistry, Indiana School of Dentistry, reports a variety of oral and dental diseases caused by smokeless tobacco.[5]

The American Cancer Society cites a recent study of women snuff users in North Carolina showing a 400 percent increase in mouth cancer.[6]

Puff or snuff, as a boy from Oregon called "Alfalfa" dis-covered: "Tobacco is not for the body."

Notes

    1. *Deseret News*, Jan. 27, 1985.

    2. *John Naisbitt's Trend Letter*, Jan. 10, 1985.

    3. *Fifty Most Often Asked Questions*, 1982, p. 38.

    4. *Time*, Feb. 4, 1985, p. 46.

    5. *Deseret News*, Feb. 1, 1985, p. B11.

    6. *Fifty Most Often Asked Questions*, p. 22.

53

Fair Farewell

The large congregation seated on the padded oak benches was hushed.

She stood erect at the oak-trimmed pulput with touches of burnt orange upholstering that matched the thick floor carpeting.

Her long, wavy, honey-hued hair reached well below her trim shoulders. She wore a well-tailored black suit with white blouse.

Her violet-blue eyes sparkled as her clear, soft voice spoke tenderly.

In her mid-thirty's, she is mother of three daughters. She had been a student body vice president at Brigham Young University and had traveled the world with its colorfully costumed folk dancers. She had been a beauty queen's attendant.

Now she resides in Woodbridge, Virginia, along the broad Potomac, some twenty-five miles south of Washington, D.C.

Terri Fisher Jensen was speaking in the West at the funeral of her father-in-law,[1] a noble builder, teacher, and missionary. He had been taken by cancer at eighty-one.

Her message was to him:

"We flew in from Washington, D.C., just a few hours ago and pulled into the long, lean lane leading to the last house you built," she began. "I looked at the kitchen table you built and recalled the many sweet memories we have made around its edges."

She spoke of the "mountain air you relished." Then added: "You and nature's quiet suited each other: both unassuming and unpretentious, each knowing that the majority of life's most significant events occur in quiet, unheralded moments. Center stage was not your spot and you didn't need the applause or approval of anyone for your own validation."

Terri spoke admiringly of the departed's companion: "Her ability to love abundantly and live faithfully blessed you always. In the end, I think she knew that faith *does* change things. But she also must have understood that sometimes it takes *more* faith to accept things as they are than it does to change them."

More feelingly she said: "I thank you for giving life to, and for raising, such an incredibly special son as Larry. He is the finest human being I have ever known, and I am proud to be his wife.

"I thank you for being a man of honor."

It was a joyous message that seemed to send people homeward wanting to live more nobly.

Funerals and death itself can be radiantly reassuring.

The great Beethoven, deaf as he neared his demise at fifty-six, exclaimed: "I shall hear in heaven."

Thomas Carlyle tells how able Queen Maria Theresa of Austria, mother of sixteen, refused to take drugs when dying. She explained: "I want to meet my God awake."

James Drummond Burns, nineteenth century hymn writer, said as his earthly end approached: "I have been dying for twenty years, now I am able to live."

To Latter-day Saints, death is but a change, as if moving from one home to another, in the wondrous, unending journey of immortality.

Said the Lord: "Those that die in me shall not taste of death, for it shall be sweet unto them." (D&C 42:46.)

Every one who ever lives on earth, the Prince of Peace and his prophets have repeatedly assured us, shall receive the blessing of a literal resurrection. (See 1 Corinthians 15:22 and Alma 11:41–42; 40:4.)

What a glorious glimpse of the tall tomorrows ahead Jesus gave us when He said to the Eleven in His twilight earthly hours:

"He that believeth on me, the works that I do shall he do also; and greater works than these shall he do; because I go unto my Father." (John 14:2.)

No wonder there seemed to be joy in that oak-trimmed chapel when a vivaciously vibrant blond mother spoke her goodbye to her quiet hero.

Indeed it was lovely—a fair farewell.

Notes

    1. Lyman Marcus Jensen.

54

From Beer to Bier

From Cleveland, Ohio, home of one of the world's great symphonies, just over a year ago came a sobering Associated Press story:[1]

A teenage girl was sentenced by a county juvenile court to "losing her driver's license for life." She also was ordered to "perform 1,040 hours of volunteer work with children."

Why the tough sentence?

Kim Weber, eighteen, was drunk when the car she was driving crashed into the rear of another car, killing two children, aged three and four.

The published article did not say what the teenager had been drinking. Chances are it was beer.

"Beer is the most popular alcohol choice among teenage drinkers," says a publication of Preferred Risk Insurance Companies.[2]

One-half to three-fourths of the auto accidents in the United States, including approximately fifty-thousand deaths a year, involve alcohol.

At what ages is drinking most likely to become involved in highway fatalities?

Studies show between seventeen and twenty, according to

William N. Plymat, Jr., Des Moines, Iowa, executive director of American Council on Alcohol Problems.

Mr. Plymat so testified before a U.S. Senate committee, chaired by Senator Paula Hawkins of Florida.[3]

The First Presidency, in a statement issued February 6, 1985, declared that the Church "joins with others calling for a ban or stringent curtailment of alcohol advertising on all media."

And with good cause.

"Sixty percent of those who die in alcohol-related crashes are between 15 and 24," reports California Council on Alcohol Problems.[4] "Alcohol is involved in more than 66 percent of the nation's homicides, 50 percent of rapes, and up to 70 percent of sexually aggressive acts against children, and assaults."

Yet the barrage of beer advertising continues on television, with tens of millions of people, particularly youth, as viewers.

More than that, big beer companies continue to move right onto college campuses with their kegs and cans and mugs and melodies promoting sales. The brewers sponsor rock concerts, senior picnics, turtle races, before-game tailgate parties, and other campus activities.

The Wall Street Journal notes that big campus promotions continue despite "the recent national law requiring states to raise the drinking age to twenty-one by 1986 to avoid losing federal highway funds."[5]

Beer advertising on television and radio in 1981 reached $426.8 million.

Per capita beer consumption climbed from 20.1 gallons in 1973 to 24.2 gallons in 1983.

"It's only beer," a teenager might say. Yet it has the same ingredient—ethyl alcohol—found in whiskey. A 12-ounce can or bottle of beer has about the same amount of alcohol as a 1½-ounce shot of whiskey.

A national survey[6] showed that 56 percent of high school students "had started drinking when they were in ninth grade or earlier."

Another poll showed that two of three college students "acknowledged that they drove a car while intoxicated."[7]

Sadly, thousands of those "two of three" became involved in a highway fatality—literally from beer to bier.

Is it worth the risk?

A wise teenager will make up his or her mind long before an offer or pressure for a beer comes:

"This beer's *not* for me, ever."

In Kirtland, in that same Cleveland area where a teenage girl received a judge's chilling sentence, the Lord spoke to a prophet 152 years ago: "Strong drinks are not for the belly." (D&C 89:7.)

Notes

1. Nov. 18, 1983.

2. *Honest Answers to Questions Teenagers Ask About Drinking,* Des Moines, Iowa.

3. Feb. 7, 1985, before the Subcommittee on Alcoholism and Drug Abuse, U.S. Senate Committee on Labor and Human Resources.

4. From "The 1982 Report on Drug Abuse and Alcoholism" by John A. Califano, former HEW Secretary.

5. Jan. 30, 1985.

6. Conducted for the National Institute on Drug Abuse, reported in *The Booze Merchants* (Washington, D.C., Center for Science and Public Interest) 1983, p. 47.

7. Ibid., p. 48.

55

Homers

William (Bill) DeBirk is a retired house painter, trim of build, with gray-brown hair and smiling, gray-blue eyes.

He was born in the Netherlands, son of a house painter, who was also son of a house painter.

Bill DeBirk came to the United States in 1953, settling in the West.

Bill raises homing pigeons for a hobby, as he did as a boy in Holland. These birds, though trucked hundreds of miles away, have an uncanny way of finding their way home. Homing pigeons carried messages for ancient Egyptians and Persians three thousand years ago, about the time David reigned in Israel.

The DeBirk's pigeon house, or loft, is in the rear of their shake-sided, frame home, with matching yellow and brown trim.

There are some twenty-four registered homing pigeons in the loft. They race for prizes with birds of other nearby breeders, generally over distances from 120 to 600 miles.

One of Bill DeBirk's pigeons failed to return to its loft in a race from Mountain Home, Idaho, in May 1983. This particular blue-gray pigeon was a year old.

That is not unusual. Pigeons, which generally fly about forty miles an hour, sometimes do not return to the loft because of hawks, bad weather, or other misfortunes.

But on February 1, 1985, nearly two years after the race, the bird returned to Bill DeBirk's loft, with its metal band bearing No. 1301 still attached to its reddish-brown leg.

"Where she has been, I have no idea," said Bill, happily. "She was required to fly over some high mountain ranges in that flight. When she returned she looked as though she had weathered some severe elements."

It is wonderful for pigeons to want to come home, like that lost homer.

It is even more heartwarming to have a home that is a happy haven for those who live there—a place where all who live there are "homers."

After Jesus had cast the demons out of a violent man and he had become calmly reverent, the Master said to him:

"Go home to thy friends, and tell them how great things the Lord hath done for thee. . . ." (Mark 15:19.)

Every person, particularly a child or teenager, deserves to return to a home where there are friends.

Home should be where a tot can go to be listened to—caringly. By a mother. A father. A sister or a brother. Better still, by all.

A teenager, away at college, recently wrote a birthday note to her mother: "I appreciate your wise counsel and understanding heart . . . to know that you will love me no matter what I do. . . . Thanks for the trust you have shown me."

Close friends of the pretty coed say she loves to go home or tell her parents on the phone whom she is dating, about her studies, Church activities, worries, hopes, and joys.

Homes with working mothers continue to increase dramatically. So do homes where a valiant mother is often the sole breadwinner. But perhaps the most precious and profitable time that mother can spend is in listening to her child.

Concerned by the alarming rise in child sexual abuse, the U.S. Human Development Services, headed by Dodie Livingston, has produced a six-page folder, *Child Sexual Abuse Prevention, Tips to Parents,* for preventing this tragedy.[1]

The folder begins: "Listen and talk with your children."

Love at home has so many rich rewards. One of them: making homers of children.

Unfortunately, there are between 1.3 and 1.5 million runaway children in the United States every year. Even more sadly, of those runaways a fast-growing portion are "throwaways" or "pushouts," according to the National Network of Runaway Youth Services.[2]

Listening at home can be the difference between a homer and a runaway.

Among pigeons, homers are exalted birds. Among people, homers are the strength of a nation and the heart of the restored Church.

Notes

1. *Child Sexual Abuse Prevention, Tips to Parents* (Washington, D.C., Office of Human Development Service, 1984), free upon request. Write U.S. Dept. of Health and Human Services, Washington, D.C. 20201.

2. Washington, D.C.

56

People's Prophet

It was springtime in the Rockies. It was morning, and there had been light snow flurries across Salt Lake Valley's greening foothills. The apricot trees, as if sprinkled with popcorn, were in bloom.

The day was Thursday, April 4, 1974.

A short, stocky, baldish man stood at the portable pulpit in the auditorium off the main lobby in the twenty-eight-story, cast-stone Church Office Building. Virtually every yellow upholstered seat was occupied.

Gathered were General Authorities, regional representatives, auxiliary leaders, and department heads.

Spencer Woolley Kimball had been leader of the Church less than a hundred days. This was his first major address as prophet and Church President. He was seventy-eight. Less than two years before, he had undergone open heart surgery. Seventeen years before, surgery had removed most of his two vocal cords because of cancer.

President Kimball's voice was labored and raspy. But he spoke for approximately sixty minutes. He spoke globally of pushing into broad new frontiers with missionary work.

He recalled a prophet-leader who lived in the Americas more than a century before the birth of Jesus:

"King Benjamin, that humble but mighty servant of the Lord, called together all the people in the land of Zarahemla, and the multitude was so great that King Benjamin 'caused a tower to be erected, that thereby his people might hear the words which he should speak unto them.' " (Mosiah 2:7.)

Then President Kimball added:

"Our Father in Heaven has now provided us with mighty towers—radio and television towers with possibilities beyond comprehension—to help fulfill the words of the Lord that 'the sound must go forth from this place unto all the world." (D&C 58:64.)

As the Church honors President Kimball on his ninetieth birthday anniversary Thursday, March 28, 1985, much can be found in common between him and ancient King Benjamin.

Both spoke powerfully through mighty towers. More importantly, both moved men and women and children to loftier lives because they were "of the people."

Mosiah records that King Benjamin labored with his own hands to serve the people (Mosiah 2:14.) In that address from the tower he declared: "When ye are in the service of your fellow beings ye are only in the service of your God." (Mosiah 2:17.)

When he was fifty-three, and had been a hard-toiling Apostle for five years, Spencer W. Kimball was stricken with a severe heart attack. To help his recovery he rode in a car for several days with a trusted friend, with a supply of food, chlorine tablets to treat contaminated water, "and a case of root beer and orange pop." They pitched camp in "a borrowed trailer-tent under some pines" among the Navajos in New Mexico. The Apostle remained two weeks.

A little sheep-tending Navajo girl taught him and a young missionary recuperating from ailing knees to count to a hundred in Navajo and to sing a Navajo song. Elder Kimball tied a ribbon around his forehead and he and the missionary sang the Navajo song to the delight of a group of Indians.

People observed that even when Spencer W. Kimball was President of the Church he would take his place in long Lion

House cafeteria lines, not allowing others to move him up front. He and his Camilla were the same in funeral home viewing lines.

His favorite food: bread and milk.

President Kimball's deeds of helpfulness are legend. As an Apostle visiting for stake conference in Lost River, Idaho, he helped his host feed cattle in sub-zero weather after a Saturday night meeting. In Rigby, Idaho, arriving at the stake president's home at 10:00 P.M. after a meeting, he slipped into overalls and milked two of three cows.

In Richfield, Utah, he drove down a deadend street to visit eight Indian families tenting in deep snow and lying under cardboard and mattresses for warmth. He helped.[1]

D. Arthur Haycock, his loyal and trusted secretary, confided that President Kimball has for years maintained a special fund— "not substantial." From it have come quiet gifts of greenbacks to troubled people who came to his office not for money but for counsel.

To hundreds of young men, in the United States and Canada, aged about twelve, he has slipped a dollar bill "for your missionary fund." In Britain, it was a pound. In Latin America, ten pesos or so.

Few leaders have accomplished so much globally in building the Kingdom of God in this century as has Spencer W. Kimball.

Like King Benjamin of old, he stands tall because he reaches out.

Notes

1. See Kimball, Edward L. and Andrew E., Jr., *Spencer W. Kimball* (Salt Lake City, Utah, Bookcraft, Inc., 1977), pp. 232–56.

57

"I Shall Rise Again!"

Just a short block north of Damascus Gate, the main entrance to walled Old Jerusalem, is a shady garden of pink roses, red geraniums, cactus plants, red poppies, and daffodils. There are also bushy pines, gray-green olive trees, lemon and pomegranate trees, and other blooms, bushes, and trees.

Carved out of a tan-gray stone wall at the lower end of the garden is a door-shaped entrance to an ancient tomb.

Here, many scholars believe, was where the miracle of the first Easter occurred. Here, they say, came a weeping Mary Magdalene early in the morning "when it was yet dark." (John 20:1.) Then it was that she met her risen Lord, He whose lifeless body had been placed in a tomb two days before.

And with that miracle came the glorious gift of an assured resurrection for every person who has ever lived on earth.

"As in Adam all die, even so in Christ shall all be made alive," (1 Corinthians 15:22) declared Paul to the Saints in ancient Corinth. Other prophets before and after Paul have affirmed that universal gift: a literal resurrection for all.

You will rise again. So will every man, woman, and child.

That is a truth upon which to reflect when trials, reverses, heartaches, and chilling defeats come.

A man loses his job or his business. A woman loses her husband to death or divorce. A cancer patient hears from his doctor the disease is terminal. A child is abused. One errs, seriously. It is often so natural to say: "This is it." Or: "This is the end of the world for me." Or: "I'm really a loser." Or: "Why should this happen to me?"

How much better to reflect on that first Easter, and say: "I shall rise again!"

Twelve years ago in a major hospital in the West, a sixtyish community leader lay on his bed near death. He had undergone major surgery for colon cancer. He had confided to loved ones that he doubted if he would last through the night.

Then near midnight he heard the hushed sounds of a prayer beside his bed. It was his surgeon, kneeling, pleading with his Heavenly Father to spare the life of his patient, a dear friend. The patient today holds a key position in the Church. His influence for good is felt broadly.

Countless are the stories of people rising from the depths.

Heber J. Geurts is a ruddy-faced, hazel-eyed man with curly, silver hair. He is stocky, only five feet four inches tall, and seventy-seven years old. Motherless at six and with an invalid father, he began hawking newspapers downtown when only eight. Later he supervised newsboys, retiring in 1982 after selling newspapers for sixty-six years.

In 1957, when he was serving as a bishop, two of his ward members were committed to the state penitentiary. Bishop Geurts did not forget them. For twenty-eight years he has been a friend to these and other inmates. For scores of them he has organized weekly family home evenings with visiting, volunteer "adopted" families.

Hebe Geurts has helped countless inmates realize: "I shall rise again!"

One of them was Ed, tall, skinny, dark-haired and pale. "He was the worst drug addict I ever dealt with," recalled Hebe Geurts. At the prison they called him "Junkie Ed." He was from the East, and served several terms, a total of some twenty-two years. About eight years ago he got involved in the family home evening program at the prison. Three years later "Junkie Ed" was released. His "adopted family" got him a job as a painter. Three years ago Bishop Geurts received a phone call from Ed. He wanted Hebe Geurts to accompany Ed and his wife to the temple. At Christmastime, Hebe received a greeting card from Ed. He is now high priests group leader.

From defeat, Ed has risen again.

Jim[1] was married with a loyal wife and five children. He was in and out of prison for some fifteen years—stealing and robbing to support his alcohol and drug habit.

Four years ago, when Hebe Geurts was walking down the prison corridor, Jim stopped him. "I'm ready," the inmate told Bishop Geurts, who had encouraged him to get involved in the Church program at the prison. After Jim was off parole, he and his wife and children were sealed in the temple. Today he is Scoutmaster and Aaronic Priesthood adviser.

Another "down-and-outer" has risen.

Surely it is true: A man, woman, or child fails only when he or she fails to realize that "I shall rise again."

Notes

1. Not his actual name.

58

Search for
the Living

Among the new Church missionaries arriving amid Hong Kong's whirring forest of skyscrapers in March, 1985 was Matthew Guy Bagley.[1]

A freshman from Brigham Young University, Matt Bagley, a trim six feet tall with dark blond hair and searching green eyes, will probably miss his cross-country skiing, American baseball and basketball, tennis, and golf.

But few young men could enter missionary service better prepared. When he was only seven, Matt decided to read all the standard works from cover to cover before he was baptized at eight. He did. For good measure, he repeated the scriptural feat by the time he was ten.

He is a proven leader, having served as student body vice president in a large high school.

When missionary preparation day comes, if Matt Bagley goes true to form, he will find his way to a Hong Kong genealogy library.

During his past ten years, Matt has spent more hours with genealogy than with athletics, student activities, eating spaghetti and chocolate ice cream, and on horses with his dentist father rounding up the family Herefords in central Utah's back country —all combined.

He has wolfed down facts and figures on his forebears as if they were chow mein, another favorite food.

He has compiled more than two thousand handwritten pages on his ancestors. He has traced his roots through ten generations. In his wondrous search he has discovered he is a descendant of England's Kings Edward I, II, and III.

For birthday gifts he has asked for biographies on the three Edwards. He has written absorbing profiles on them.

Edward I became England's king in 1272, the year after Marco Polo of Venice began his long and storied travels across Asia. Edward I conquered Wales, won historic victories in Scotland, established a model parliament, and sponsored laws aimed at destroying the feudal system and limiting the power of the church. He was one of Britain's great monarchs.

Matt feasted on such facts about his forebears, whom he traced also into Norway, Denmark, and Switzerland. He studied paperbacks on languages of these lands.

Rooting for his roots gave him a thirst for American history, too. He memorized all the United States presidents in order. Once for Halloween trick-or-treat he dressed not as a ghost but as a favorite president: Ulysses S. Grant.

Matt has guided eleven or twelve teenage friends into the joys of genealogical research.

One of the highlights of his life came when he was thirteen. On an evening in the Manti Temple, atop a hill of cream-white oolite rock of which the edifice is built, Matt gathered with his parents, grandparents, sister, and aunt and uncle.

There in radiant white they performed temple ordinances for a family of Danish forebears, with Matt talking warmly about them as though they were next of kin. He performed the vicarious baptisms.

For Matthew Guy Bagley, genealogy is not "searching out the dead." It is an exciting adventure of seeking the living who have moved on. It is looking for one's own, finding them, and getting acquainted with them. It is a wonderful world of giving—bringing to those whose records have been found the priceless gift of sacred and vital temple ordinances.

Today much of the search can be done through the archives of the Church: the world's largest collection of genealogical records, with an estimated 1.4 billion names. The Church operates some 550 branch genealogical libraries in twenty-four countries. The libraries are usually listed in the local telephone directory, in the yellow pages under "Churches."

You, too, can join people like Matt Bagley in today's adventure that brings renewed meaning to the Apostle Paul's questions to the Saints in ancient Corinth, the mighty city with harbors on both sides of a narrow Greek isthmus:

"Else what shall they do which are baptized for the dead, if the dead rise not at all? why are they then baptized for the dead?" (1 Corinthians 15:29.)

Notes

    1. Son of Lell O. and Carol Baker Bagley.

59

Loving the Lord in Lahore

If you shot an arrow directly through the earth entering at Salt Lake City, the arrow would probably emerge near Lahore (pronounced Luh-*hohr*) in Pakistan.

Lahore's time is exactly twelve hours different from the Mountain West's. When it is 9:00 A.M. in Salt Lake City, it is 9:00 P.M. in Lahore.

Lahore is Pakistan's second (to Karachi) largest city, with a population of more than two million. It has many landmarks recalling the Mogul Empire, which was founded in the 1500s and which gave to the world the wondrous Taj Mahal in Agra, some four hundred miles away in India.

Lahore lies in a rich farming area and is a weaving center.

Pakistan today is 97 percent Muslim, while India, of which Pakistan was once part, is mostly Hindu.

Each Sabbath in a three-bedroom, white plaster home with slightly sloping roof in Lahore, between twenty and thirty people gather for a branch sacrament meeting of the Church. Some of the brown-skinned Pakistani men come in white pantaloons with loose, white tunics. Other attenders wear western dress.

About half are members of the Church—mostly Americans in government service there. The others are Pakistanis, mostly Christian.

Presiding is black-haired, sturdy Max G. Williams, fifty-nine years of age and an irrigation engineer. He, with the U.S. State Department's Agency of International Development, is helping Pakistanis improve their crop watering (mostly rice in the summer, wheat in the winter).

That sacrament meeting in the home of Max and Barbara Dahl Williams is one of two known to be held regularly in Pakistan, with a population of some 95 million. Another branch sacrament meeting in Pakistan is held at Islamabad, the country's capital. There is not a functioning stake or mission of the Church within 1,500 miles of Lahore.

Few, if any, members of the Church have attended sacrament meetings regularly in so many widely scattered, remote areas of the world in the past eight years as have Barbara and Max Williams: in Turkey, Bangladesh, Iran, Peru, Indonesia, and now Pakistan.

Usually the authorized meetings have been held in their home.

In Lahore there are hymns, the sacrament, a lesson on gospel principles, and prayers. Sacrament meeting is followed by a joint priesthood and Relief Society session.

To the Williamses, sacrament meetings are precious. They "are the most solemn and sacred meetings in the Church."[1]

The first meeting of the restored Church was actually the first sacrament meeting. On that Tuesday, April 6, 1830, some fifty to sixty men and women crowded into Peter Whitmer, Sr.'s, two-room, log farmhouse with a slanted roof and tiny attic. They had come by horseback, wagon, and foot to this Fayette township home in western New York's wilderness.

Six young men participated in the organization of the Church, under the leadership of the Prophet Joseph Smith. Ordinances were performed. The sacrament was blessed as had been directed by the Lord. (See D&C 20:76–79.)

Partaking of the sacrament is the sacred privilege of each Church member every Sabbath to renew his or her covenant with the Lord made at the time of baptism.

Nothing binds one to the Church like sacrament meeting.

The sacrament was instituted by the Lord Himself with His Apostles in an upper room in Jerusalem on the occasion of the Feast of the Passover.

The sacrament is a pause for remembrance, rededication, and renewal.

Blessed are they, like Barbara and Max Williams, who unfailingly attend sacrament meeting each week regardless of where in the world they go.

More and more Latter-day Saints continue to realize that truth.

In 1920, when Church membership totaled 526,032, the percent of members attending sacrament meeting on a given Sunday was 19. In 1960, with 1,693,180 members, the percentage was 34.

In 1984, with approximately 5,400,000 members, 42.8 percent attended sacrament meeting on a given day.

Church membership since 1920 has increased slightly over ten times, but sacrament meeting attendance has climbed 23.7 times!

Around the globe, from La Paz to London, from Los Angeles to Lisbon, there are Saints like the little group in Lahore. They draw nearer to the Lord and to each other weekly as they "remember him and keep his commandments . . . that they may always have his Spirit to be with them." (D&C 20:77.)

Notes

1. McConkie, Bruce R., *Mormon Doctrine* (Salt Lake City, Utah, Bookcraft, Inc., 1958), p. 595.

60

Teach by the Spirit

It all began in the 105-year-old, twenty-three-spired Assembly Hall, built on Temple Square of gray granite left over from the construction of its big sister, the great Salt Lake Temple.

It was the first session of what was really two worldwide conferences wedded into one:

• The 155th Annual General Conference of the Church.

• A conference of the 188, plus 60 newly called, mission presidents, and their wives.

Outside the Assembly Hall on that Wednesday, April 3, 1985, an early spring day, the pansies, some maroon and others white, smiled from their beds in the afternoon sunshine.

Inside on the oak benches sat mission presidents and wives newly arrived from their fields—from Jamaica and Japan, Korea and Kentucky, Africa West and Alaska, Fiji and Finland, and from scores of other lands.

Speaker after speaker spoke of a revelation received 154 years ago by the Prophet Joseph Smith, then only twenty-six years old, in Kirtland, Ohio: "He that receiveth the word by the Spirit of truth receiveth it as it is preached by the Spirit of truth." (D&C 50:21.)

In that first session of the mission presidents' conference, President Ezra Taft Benson began a powerful address based on a review of missionary messages of President Spencer W. Kimball. Declared President Benson:

"It's the Spirit that counts!"

There in the Assembly Hall, General Authorities announced an improved plan of discussions for missionaries. The emphasis now will be: "Teach by the Spirit." Memorized discussions will be replaced by those allowing the missionary to let his or her personal testimony surface more. There will be more listening to the investigator.

One leader explained:

"Let the Holy Ghost do the teaching, with the missionary as the instrument." Elder Boyd K. Packer stressed that conversion comes through the power of the Spirit.

In his welcoming remarks, President Gordon B. Hinckley read a letter from a missionary to his family, showing power from the Spirit. The elder described baptizing a 265-pound man confined to a wheelchair. "I felt some help carrying him" to the font, the elder wrote. "I've never felt so good. Better than football even."

One of the great discourses of the general conference, and of many conferences, was that of ailing (with cancer) Elder Bruce R. McConkie. He described in vivid detail events surrounding the crucifixion and resurrection of Jesus Christ.

Elder McConkie's message was a masterful model of "teaching by the Spirit."

He concluded his classic with his personal witness:

"In a coming day I shall feel the nail marks in his hands and in his feet and shall wet his feet with my tears."

Then, like a great organ sounding powerfully from pallid pipes, he affirmed:

"But I shall not know any better then than I know now that he is God's Almighty Son."[1]

There were tributes during the two-in-one conference to Presiding Bishop Victor L. Brown, released after thirteen years in that key position and twenty-four years in the Presiding Bishopric. Particular mention was made of his leadership with the worldwide building program of the Church. It was noted that

some one thousand meetinghouses are now under construction—
to accommodate the Church's growth, both natural and convert.
(President Hinckley reported 192,983 convert baptisms in 1984,
"The equivalent of sixty-four new stakes.")

Gratitude was also given the valiant, newly released counselors in the Presiding Bishopric: H. Burke Peterson and J.
Richard Clarke.

All three members of the released Bishopric were called to the
First Quorum of the Seventy and given new assignments.

Named new Presiding Bishop was Elder Robert D. Hales, a
General Authority for ten years. He was a seasoned high-level
executive with several big U.S. corporations. His counselors are
Henry B. Eyring, who has been Church commissioner of education; and Glenn L. Pace, manager of Church welfare services.

The global "teaching by the Spirit" was underlined in the call
of three stalwart natives of widely scattered areas to the First
Quorum of the Seventy:

Hans Benjamin Ringger, electrical engineer and architect born
in Zurich, Switzerland.

Waldo Pratt Call, Sr., born in Colonia Juarez, Mexico,
orchardist and high school teacher.

Helio da Rocha Camargo, native of Resende, Brazil, and a
farmer since retiring as a Brazilian army officer.

Elder William Grant Bangerter, whose younger brother
Norman is governor of Utah, was called to succeed the late Elder
G. Homer Durham in the Presidency of the First Quorum of the
Seventy.

It was an historic double conference on flowered, sun-
showered Temple Square at Eastertide.

The theme was clear and timely. In spreading the gospel in the
home, the classroom, in missionary service, or wherever, it is
better to "teach by the Spirit."

Notes

1. *Ensign*, May 1985, p. 11.

61

Golden Year of Giving

"On the scrubby lawn before a dingy gray cottage in Salt Lake City, Utah, two tattered, underfed children were fashioning mud pies one day last week.

"In the bare kitchen they knew no sweets and pastries were a-making, for the weary mother had naught but the plainest food to cook, and little of that.

"For two long years the family, like thousands of others, had existed on public funds.

"Suddenly, the rickety gate swung open, and from the broad, shady street stepped a smiling ward teacher of the Mormon Church.

"Into the household he went, the curious youngsters at his heels; he brought the welcome news that the Church was taking over their support, and that gradually it would assume responsibility for all of its eighty-eight-thousand members now on relief. By October 1, he told them, there would be no Mormons on the dole."

So began a full-page article, illustrated with a picture of the Salt Lake Temple, in *Literary Digest*,[1] then one of America's leading magazines. Similar articles appeared in *Time*, the Washington *Post*, New York *Times*, and other publications.

That was in May and June, 1936, as the world struggled out of the Great Depression.

Only two or three weeks before these articles appeared, stout, jut-jawed Benito Mussolini's invading Italian troops had occupied Addis Ababa, Ethiopia's capital.

Now as the Church enters the fiftieth year of its welfare services program, *USA Today*[2] headlined an article: "Fasters Raise Famine Funds." The story told of a special fast in the United States and Canada, called by the First Presidency, to provide funds for starving people in Ethiopia and other African countries. *USA Today* reported more than $6 million was collected through the fast. The donations would be used for food, medicine, tents (30,000 of them), and efforts to drill for water.

Welfare services in 1936 and today aims to help the needy to help themselves. At the first welfare services regional meeting forty-nine years ago, President Heber J. Grant deplored laziness. "We want our people to work and to work earnestly," he said.[3]

Actually from the beginnings of the restored Church there has been a welfare program.

In a revelation to the Prophet Joseph Smith in Fayette, New York, where the Church had been organized nine months before, the Lord said:

"Certain men . . . shall be appointed . . . and they shall look to the poor and the needy, and administer to their relief that they shall not suffer." (D&C 38:34—35.)

Caring for others has been a teaching of the Lord since early times. To ancient Israel, He declared: "Thou shalt love thy neighbour as thyself." (Leviticus 19:18.) To the rich man, Jesus said: "Give to the poor, and thou shalt have treasure in heaven." (Mark 10:21.)

Much could be written about far-flung farms, canneries, and well-stocked storehouses—all part of welfare services. But the aim of the program, in the words of Bishop Glenn L. Pace of the Presiding Bishopric (for four years managing director of welfare services), "the objective is getting an individual on his own feet."

One such person was a woman in her eighties in an Idaho nursing home, "the only member of the Church in her family."

She was suffering with painful cancer—two-hundred-dollars worth of pain medication every month."

A ward Relief Society leader brought her two dolls to clean up, fix their hair, and make new dresses for them. They were for needy children for Christmas.

A few weeks later, the Relief Society leader returned. The two dolls had been cleaned and attractively dressed. The elderly woman also had made eleven baby quilts for the poor.

Seven more dolls were brought to the elderly woman. Beautiful bonnets, dresses, and coats were made for six of them. The woman died before the seventh doll was outfitted. Her family found her diary. An entry read:

"3:00 A.M., couldn't sleep, the pain was intense. Decided to work on the dolls, and the pain went away."

Entry after entry repeated: "Decided to work on the dolls, and the pain went away."

In Ethiopia or Idaho, Church Welfare Services, entering its golden year, continues to help people "stand on their own feet."

As with a pain-ridden woman in a nursing home, the program also brings to life the lines of Jesus to the Twelve as He sent them out to teach: "He that loseth his life for my sake shall find it." (Matthew 10:39.)

Notes

1. June 6, 1936.
2. April 8, 1985.
3. *Millennial Star*, London, England, May 21, 1936, p. 327.

62

Garden for Greatness

Tucked amid the mesquite-covered hills of old Mexico some 150 miles southwest of El Paso are two towns that are uniquely different for Mexico.

Venerable red brick homes, often two-story and with white trim, are there. Dusty streets line the towns' square blocks.

Adobe structures and plodding burros are not hallmarks there, but there are holstein and jersey cows and high-stepping saddle horses.

Pink-cheeked tots, some freckled, scamper across the lawns. Basketball hoops hang on barns and garages. For nearly a century a Church-operated academy, now confined to classes for junior and senior high school levels, has trained the youth of the area.

Apples and peaches are the main crops in the two towns.

The older of the towns is Colonia Jaurez, situated in a narrow valley and bordered by high bluffs. It was founded in 1885 by a group of Latter-day Saints under Canadian-born Isaac Turley of Arizona.

Fifteen miles northeast of Colonia Jaurez is its sister town, Colonia Dublan. It was also settled in the late 1880s by Latter-day Saints from the Rocky Mountains, seeking a haven from harassment because of plural marriage.

Juarez Stake, comprised of Mormon colonies in the area, was organized December 9, 1895. The first stake president was Anthony Woodward Ivins, a buckskin-loving cattleman, Church and political leader, and explorer.

"Tony" Ivins became First Counselor in the First Presidency to President Heber J. Grant.

After President Ivins, greatness has streamed out of the Juarez colonies like honeybees out of a hive. Perhaps no area of the Church since the great Mormon exodus from Nauvoo has produced so many giants of achievement from so few people.

Here are but a few of the mighty men and women who have been raised there:

Marion G. Romney, First Counselor in the First Presidency.

Henry Eyring, for decades an internationally eminent chemist and Church leader.

Camilla Eyring Kimball, wife of President Spencer W. Kimball.

George Romney, one of America's top automotive industrialists of the twentieth century, once a member of the United States Cabinet, Regional Representative, and stake president.

Franklin S. Harris, who served as president of both Utah State University and Brigham Young University. (While not a native of the Juarez colonies, he moved there as a lad with his parents and grew up there.)

Carl F. Eyring, nationally eminent scientist (Bell Telephone) and for many years dean of BYU's College of Arts and Sciences.

Joseph T. Bentley, general superintendent, Young Men's Mutual Improvement Association (1958–62).

Waldo Pratt Call, Sr., orchardist, who was sustained a member of the First Quorum of the Seventy in April 1985.

A refining experience for the Juarez colonists came during the Mexican Revolution (1910–1916). The colonists were caught between government and rebel armies. Several thousand of the colonists fled Mexico for the United States at that time. Many later returned.

Six times in one night in 1915 groups of armed men entered the large brick home of Anson B. Call, where five other families had gathered. The soldiers, pushing the occupants around at gunpoint, took food, clothing, and bedding. The women and children were ordered upstairs; the men and older boys, in the kitchen.

After gathering their loot, one of the intruders laughed that they would now "go upstairs and take care of the women."

Hearing the remark, Brother Call, who was to serve as bishop of Dublan Ward for twenty-nine years, moved to the foot of the stairs.

"Don't go up there," said he, a slim farmer-businessman with thin, brown hair.

"Who is going to stop us?" was the reply.

"I am," said Bishop Call. "If you go up there you go over my dead body." Then in the power of the priesthood, he rebuked them. Guns were lowered. The intruders departed the home "like whipped dogs," leaving behind the pillow slips loaded with loot.

Such is the stuff of which the people of the Mexican colonies are made.

From those "twin towers of testimony" has come much of the leadership for the remarkable growth of the Church in Mexico in recent years.

In the past thirty years, thirty-four men born and reared in Juarez Stake have served as mission presidents—mostly in Latin America.

Beginning in May and continuing into August will be a centennial celebration in Colonia Juarez and Colonia Dublan. There will be firesides, outings, marathon race, parade, rodeo, pageant, and special Church services.

Those who have come from there as well as those whose roots are there can be proud. The Juarez colonies indeed have been "a garden for greatness" in the kingdom of God.

63

Hands That Link
with Heaven

A few weeks ago an article[1] that dominated two pages in the New York *Times* was headlined:

"Laying On of Hands Gains New Respect."

The article reported studies showing therapeutic benefits through the laying on of hands.

To Latter-day Saints the blessings that come from the laying on of hands are far greater than therapeutic.

Since ancient times one of the greatest of all gifts—receiving the Holy Ghost—has come through the laying on of hands. The scriptures record how the resurrected Jesus gave that gift to His chosen twelve disciples in the Western Hemisphere. (See 3 Nephi 18:36–37; Moroni 2:1–3.)

The holy priesthood, the authority to act in the name of God, has been conferred through the laying on of hands since the days of Adam. (See D&C 84:6–17.)

Patriarchal blessings, settings apart of officers in the Church, fathers' blessings to their children, and blessings to the sick are all conferred through the laying on of hands.

Jesus put His hands on little children and on the afflicted and blessed them. (See Mark 6:5, 10:16; Luke 13:10–13.) The sick were healed.

In this day, nationally respected leaders have affirmed the spiritual gifts coming through blessings with the laying on of hands from priesthood holders in the restored Church.

Thomas Leiper Kane was a prominent Philadelphia attorney who moved among the highest government circles in Washington, D.C.

He spent much of the summer of 1846 with the Mormon refugees along the Missouri River.

Before departing, Kane asked for a blessing. Wilford Woodruff escorted him to the tent of John Smith. He had been ordained a patriarch by his nephew, Joseph the Prophet, shortly before the martyrdom.

John Smith laid his hands on Thomas L. Kane's head, and gave him a blessing, in which he said: "Thy name shall be had in honorable remembrance among the Saints to all generations."

Kane kept a copy of that blessing until his death thirty-seven years later. To this day he is honored as a champion of the Mormon people through several decades.[2]

Few American clergymen have been as well-known and respected in the twentieth century as Norman Vincent Peale, for many years editor of *Guideposts* and author of numerous books, including the best seller, *The Power of Positive Thinking*.

Ten years ago, in a syndicated radio address, Dr. Peale related:

"I had a difficulty with which I had been struggling for two or three weeks. . . . I went to speak in Salt Lake City, Utah, and was invited . . . to be received by the President of the Church and his two associate presidents. . . . The present president is Spencer W. Kimball. . . . There were these three dedicated Christian leaders—President Kimball, President N. Eldon Tanner, and President Marion G. Romney. We had a pleasant conversation and finally, at the close, I said to the President, because I thought he was so deeply spiritual, 'President Kimball, will you bless me?'

"He replied, 'You mean you want me to give you a blessing such as I give our people?'

"I said, 'Yes.'

"So he came around behind me with the other two presidents and they put their hands on my head and President Kimball in his quiet, sincere, loving manner prayed for me by name. He asked the Lord to be near me and love me and to take care of me and to guide me. As he prayed, I began to be very broken up and touched. . . .

"We said goodbye; I walked out into that crisp, sun-kissed morning. . . . And as I walked along, I suddenly felt the burden lift and I saw the answer to the difficulty and I felt the victory."

One day some parents came to the office of Elder Matthew Cowley of the Council of the Twelve. They carried a five-year-old son.

The parents said they had been fasting for two days. They said the child was born blind, deaf, and mute. They brought him for a blessing.

Elder Cowley placed his hands on the head of the child and blessed him.

A few weeks later the Apostle received a letter from the parents. They wrote:

"Brother Cowley, we wish you could see our little boy now. He is crawling. When we throw a ball across the floor, he races after it on his hands and knees. He can see. . . . He can hear."[3] (Elder Cowley died in 1953.)

Laying on of hands is indeed a link with heaven. With faith, with fasting, with righteous living, the ordinance can lift lives gloriously. It can even make miracles.

Notes

1. March 26, 1985, authored by Jane E. Brody.

2. See Ashton, Wendell J., *Theirs Is the Kingdom* (Salt Lake City, Utah, Bookcraft, Inc., 1970), p. 176.

3. Talk by Elder Matthew Cowley at BYU, 1953.

64

Lift from the Sea

Captiva Island pokes northward like a sliver of paradise from a longer, much more plump island: Sanibel. Captiva is some four miles long; Sanibel, seven.

They lie off south Florida's west coast.

The narrow road across Captiva is often festooned with huge-trunked, spreading Australian pines with their feathery, plume-line limbs. The island is lush also with both bushy and tall, lordly palms and with heavily rooted mangrove trees with leaves the size and shape of saucers. Bright red hibiscus and yellows, too, are there. So are flowering trees.

But Captiva and Sanibel are best-known for their sea shells. They are strewn like spiraled and fan-shaped jewels across the broad beaches of powdery, gray-white sand.

Here on Captiva Island, Anne Morrow Lindbergh, a mother of six on vacation in the mid-1950s, found the setting for her best-selling *Gift from the Sea.*

Here she discovered the snail shell that "sits curled up like a cat in the hollow of my hand."[1] She contemplated the moon shell and others. Delicately and graphically, she pondered with her pen "how to remain whole in the midst of distractions; how to remain balanced."²

Jesus found balance and strength in men close to the sea. The first three of His Apostles He called away from their fishing nets. They were Peter, the big fisherman of Capernaum; and James and John, gallant sons of Zebedee, who also drew their nets on Galilee.

Jesus called them to become "fishers of men." (See Matthew 4:18–22.)

As fishers of men they found new joy, a lift from life's sea. Peter became a giant of the Lord and wrote gloriously of his experiences in the service of the Master. (See 2 Peter 1:16–19.)

John as a fisher of men wrote of the great love of Jesus and of that wondrous day when "we shall be like him." (1 John 3:2; 4:16.)

Thousands of Latter-day Saint couples each year enjoy the adventures of "fishers of men."

One blond, blue-eyed Latter-day Saint mother of five invited her nonmember neighbor to a stake women's aerobics class about four years ago. Questions about the Church followed. Then the husbands got involved. Later, missionaries: one a neighbor seventy; the other, a full-time proselyting elder.

The investigators several weeks later phoned their neighbors long distance to tell them of their decision to be baptized. (The neighbors were visiting a relative some one hundred miles away.)

"It was absolute elation for us when our neighbor couple joined the Church," said the husband. "And that feeling returns every time our convert friend bears his testimony in fast meeting."

A single woman who today teaches school served as a full-time missionary in Britain. There she led seven souls into the Church.

But, she recalls, no thrill was quite like that which came later. As a volunteer guide at the Beehive House, she introduced the restored gospel to a Cuban-born elementary school teacher from Florida and his family.

"My heart is full," the volunteer guide wrote in her diary after witnessing the sealing in the temple of the Florida family of six.

The "lift from the sea" returned a few years later when she attended the temple marriage for one of the daughters.

Today there is a home teacher who not once brought a convert into the Church as a full-time missionary in England. But he baptized into the Church his former home teaching companion's wife when she was in her eighty's.

This home teacher then felt a kinship with Peter, James, and John, the original "fishers of men."

Indeed the man, now white-haired, found his Captiva Island, his "lift from the sea."

You can too, again and again, with each assist of a soul into the gospel net.

Notes

1. Lindbergh, Anne Morrow, *Gift from the Sea* (New York, N.Y., Panther Books, Inc., 1955), p. 39.

2. Ibid., p. 29.

65

Measuring the Man

It was a simmering, shimmering time in America in 1844.

The simmer was in politics. Feelings on slavery continued to heat up. The abolitionists were crusading hard against slavery.

America's shimmer in 1844 came from its emerging literary lights. Their pens were matching the brilliant poetry and prose of Victorian authors such as Dickens, Tennyson and Browning.

Interestingly, most of those Americans giving the world the glitter of their lines in the 1840s had been born in that rocky corner of the United States called New England. And in the decade of 1800—1809.

There was poet John Greenleaf Whittier, a poor Quaker farm boy born in Haverhill, Massachusetts, in 1807.

And there was Oliver Wendell Holmes, the professor who wrote elegant poetry and prose, born in Cambridge, Massachusetts, in 1807.

Also, Ralph Waldo Emerson, essayist and poet, who was born in Boston, Massachusetts, in 1803.

Nathaniel Hawthorne, author of the great novel *The Scarlet Letter*, was born in Salem, Massachusetts, in 1804; and Henry

Wadsworth Longfellow, most popular American poet of the 1800s, in Portland, Maine, in 1807.

On Thursday, June 27, 1844, out on America's frontier in Illinois, death came to another impressive figure who had been born in New England in that same decade of 1800–1809.

He was Joseph Smith, the Mormon prophet.

In the two-story, stone-walled, gable-roofed Carthage Jail, Joseph Smith and his elder brother Hyrum were slain by an armed mob with faces painted black.

How do you measure Joseph Smith today, 141 years after his martyrdom?

Interest in the subject has intensified with the surfacing of letters said to have been penned by or about him in the beginning days of the Church.

A logical method of measuring is the way people appraise those men of letters who were born in the same New England and same decade as was Joseph Smith.

Emerson and the others are measured by their works.

Joseph Smith gave to the world three notable books: the Book of Mormon, first published in 1830 when he was twenty-four, the Doctrine and Covenants, issued five years later; and the Pearl of Great Price, first printed in 1851, seven years after his death at thirty-eight.

The Book of Mormon has been available for scholars to study and weigh for 155 years. Approximately 25 million copies have been printed in thirty-nine different languages.

In 1979 the Church published a new edition of the King James Version of the Bible; two years later, new editions of the Book of Mormon, the Doctrine and Covenants and the Pearl of Great Price.

These four new editions are now available in one volume — complete with extensive dictionaries, topical guide, and foot-notes. Chapter by chapter, they are cross-referenced. The topical guide, alone, covers 598 pages with 3,495 entries.

There they are, for the world to study, probe, and compare. There they are for measuring Joseph Smith.

There can be only two logical conclusions:

1. Joseph Smith was a fraud —

or

2. He was a prophet of God, the modern revelator of Jesus Christ, the instrument through whom the savior restored His Church in this day.

If Joseph Smith was a fraud, he was a superb genius. For example, check the fifteen-page Book of Abraham in the new edition of the Pearl of Great Price. There are numerous cross-references to the Bible, Book of Mormon and the Doctrine and Covenants. If Joseph Smith was a fraud, how did he write to make everything harmonize with the Bible on the life of a prophet who lived approximately four thousand years ago?

Among those who do not accept Joseph Smith as a prophet there has emerged no consensus, no enduring explanation on how his genius produced the three books that mesh so remarkably well with thousands of biblical details.

Indeed, by the measure of his written works, Joseph Smith was a prophet, a great prophet.

Today millions of Latter-day Saints around the world gratefully sing the lines of William W. Phelps, who was a speaker at Joseph Smith's funeral in 1844:

"Praise to the man who communed with Jehovah!"[1]

Notes

1. *Hymns,* no. 149.

66

As Warm as All Outdoors

"One of the glories of our planet" is the Great Barrier Reef.

It stretches like a strand of tiny, rainbow-hued beads for more than 1,200 miles along Australia's notheast coast. Among the 2,500 reefs and 300 species of coral are as many colors and shapes as you would find in a huge Sydney toy shop.

The Coral Sea waters that wash the reef are clear and warm as a desert sky.

Near the reef's southern tip is tiny, forested Fairfax Island. It teems with harbor herons and frigate birds, skillful fliers that can hardly walk and cannot swim.

Kenneth MacLeish, then one of *National Geographic* magazine's editors, visited Fairfax Island some time ago.[1]

On Fairfax Island, the editor found an old friend, blond, sun-browned Julie Booth. She had lived alone on the island "for most of seven years."

Surprisingly, he found her Quonset hut much as it was when he passed that way five years before—surprising because at least two vicious cyclones had since ripped through.

Julie was collecting specimens and observing reef life for the Australian Museum and other institutions.

Though she was living alone, Julie continued to practice that warm hospitality typical of Australians.

As the editor approached Julie's hut, he was greeted by a dog-shaped bird. Inside was a dark, long-beaked heron. Julie called the bird Sassie, and Sassie pecked at Julie's flashing needles as she knitted and talked.

As they walked out on the beach, Julie asked her visitor to wait and watch. She waved, and hundreds of birds came, circling and soaring above her.

"You see, they come to me," she explained, "and when a storm's due, they fly round the hut and warn me with a special cry."

Australian neighborliness on the Great Barrier Reef!

Australia indeed is noted for its hospitality. Strangers are welcomed there as perhaps no other place in the world. Today approximately 20 percent of Australia's population were born in other countries. In the first thirty-five years after World War II, the Aussies welcomed some 4.5 million immigrants.

Half of them came from the British Isles. Others came from continental Europe, Latin America, and the Far East.

Among the recent immigrants are the Orrego family, from Argentina. There are now approximately five hundred Latin members of the Church living in the Sydney area. There are a Spanish-speaking ward and a Spanish-speaking branch in greater Sydney. The ward was previously presided over by Julio Orrego, father of five and color consultant for a paint and wallpaper company. His father, Allam Orrego, presides over the branch.

"Our people are so happy to be here, enjoying the freedom," reports the younger Orrego. "Australia is a very open country."

Newcomers to Australia are happy because of the hospitality of couples like Thelma and John Hobby, longtime residents of Adelaide, a big city with lush parks in South Australia. Strangers to the city without a place to stay usually have found a welcome and a bed at the modest frame Hobby home. And while brown-haired, sturdy Sister Hobby, for many years Adelaide stake Relief Society president, was serving in this role, Brother Hobby was doing his own good thing: voluntarily doing fix-up house repairs for neighbors.

Maisie Howe, a Relief Society leader in South Australia,

before driving her car into the outback (sparsely populated interior), would pray before each trip. She would pray not so much for herself as for the people and animals she might encounter on the dusty roads. (Only about one-fourth of Australia's some 510,000 miles of roads are paved.)

Australians love their great outdoors.

From the Great Coral Reef to the vast deserts of the continent's west, Australians are as warm as all outdoors. There are millions of newcomers there, but few strangers, fewer unwelcomed.

Opportunities are great for welcoming strangers by Latter-day Saints around the world.

The Lord's words to the Israelites under Moses are so well exemplified in Australia today:

"But the stranger that dwelleth with you shall be unto you as one born among you, and thou shalt love him as thyself." (Leviticus 19:34.)

Notes

1. MacLeish, Kenneth, "Exploring Australia's Coral Jungle," *National Geographic*, National Geographic Society, Washington, D.C., June 1973, pp. 742–79.

67

Tender Ties

It was only proper that her name was Abigail.

Her father, William Smith, was a Massachusetts minister. Parson Smith's mother was named Abigail.

And besides, Abigail was a good, solid biblical name. Ancient Abigail was the wife of Nabal of Carmel, rich in sheep and goats. She was "a woman of good understanding, and of a beautiful countenance." (1 Samuel 25:3.) On the death of Nabal, she married mighty David.

Abigail Smith Adams is the only woman who was both wife and mother of a president of the United States.

But she was much more. She was a model wife and mother (of five), an able manager of a large farm while her husband, John Adams, was away serving as one of America's founding lawmakers and diplomats. She could milk a cow, but she could also hold her own intellectually in Europe's most sophisticated courts.

Abigail loved the Lord, and lived and taught a lofty moral code. But she had the courage of a lioness. With thousands of letters, she fought slavery as unchristian and urged independence for the American colonies when others hesitated.

Unschooled as a lively, open-eyed child, Abigail, as a wife, feasted on Boston's four newspapers, the Bible, Shakespeare, Addison, Pope, Richardson, and others. She also crusaded hard for better education for women as molders of tomorrow's citizens. Her pointed, persuasive pen urged the nation's patriots to "remember the ladies"—not treat them as second-class citizens.

On Independence Day, Americans and people everywhere can solemnly give thanks for women like Abigail Adams.

It is true that the Lord "raised up unto this very purpose" wise men to frame the basic laws of the United States. (D&C 101:80.) But we must never forget that there were noble, God-fearing women who guided them in their boyhood, buoyed them in building a new nation.

She was married to John Adams for fifty-four years. During that time his "most trusted confidante, counselor, and defender"[1] was his beloved Abigail. To each other, they were equals with different roles.

In her letters from Britain, where John was minister during 1785–88, Abigail stressed that America could not be great without being good. Abigail could write with both candor and love, as she did in a letter to her thirteen-year-old son, John Quincy, future U.S. president and at the time a university student in Holland:

"I hope, my dear Boy that the universal Neatness and Cleanliness, of the people where you reside, will cure you of all your slovenly Tricks, and that you will learn from them Industery, Economy, and Frugality."[2]

Abigail and Thomas Jefferson respected each other's intellect immensely. But she differed with him forcibly over Shays's Rebellion in Boston in 1786. She abhorred anarchy. He said: "I like a little rebellion now and then."

While Abigail could write with frankness, she could pen with praise and warmth, as she did about Martha and George Washington. Of the First Lady, Abigail wrote to her older sister, Mary S. Cranch:

"Her Hair is white, her Teeth beautifull, her person rather short . . . Her manners are modest and unassuming, dignified, and femenine. . . . A most becoming pleasentness sits upon her countanance."

Abigail referred to President Washington as "His Majesty" and wrote of him:

"He has dignity which forbids Familiarity mixed with an easy affibility which creates Love and Reverence."[3]

When Abigail Adams died at seventy-four, Thomas Jefferson consoled John Adams by writing of the hereafter, when there will be "an ecstatic meeting with the friends we have loved and lost and whom we shall still love and never lose again."[4]

Adams replied to Jefferson:

"I believe in God and in his Wisdom and Benevolence: and I cannot conceive that such a Being could make such a Species as the human merely to live and die on this Earth. If I did not believe in a future State, I should believe in no God. . . .

"And if there be a future State, Why should the Almighty dissolve forever all the tender Ties which Unite Us so delightfully in this World . . . ?"[5]

Because Abigail and John Adams enjoyed enduring "tender ties," both were much greater. And America's beginnings were more warm and glorious.

Notes

1. Akers, Charles W., *Abigail Adams, an American Woman* (Boston, Mass., Little, Brown, and Company, 1980.) (See jacket flaps.)

2. May 26, 1781. See Peabody, James Bishop, *John Adams, a Biography in His Own Words* (New York, N.Y., *Newsweek*, 1973), vol. 2, p. 282.

3. June 28 and July 12, 1789. See ibid, pp. 338–39.

4. *Ibid.*, p. 404.

5. *Ibid.*, p. 405.

68

The Nobility of Trust

A great nation has been shaken.

It has been betrayed.

United States Defense Secretary Casper Weinberger solemnly acknowledged "very serious losses that went on over a long period of time."

He was referring to the case of the Walkers: John, his son Michael, and others charged with espionage for the Soviet Union. Key secrets on naval operations and weaponry have been sold for a series of handsome prices, it is reported.

Since 1975 a total of thirty-eight Americans have been indicted for espionage; twenty-one have been convicted. In the prior decade not one American was arrested for spying.

Wrote *Time:*

"Suddenly, ordinary Americans seemed all too willing to betray their country, not for idealogy, as in Stalin's early days, but for money, prestige and thrills."[1]

Breaking a trust goes beyond international headlines. Unfortunately there are betrayals at home. A husband breaks a trust with his companion and children. He lets them down. An employee entrusted with funds stoops to steal for "money, prestige, and thrills." Someone to whom a troubled soul has gone for counsel violates a confidence. A child tells a lie to avoid punishment. A teenager breaks a trust to avoid facing a problem and creates a bigger one by not being true to self or friend.

Gossip often is the spigot through which broken confidences flow.

The Apostle Paul wrote to young Timothy, whom Paul called his own "son in the faith":

"O Timothy, keep that which is committed to thy trust." (1 Timothy 6:20.)

George MacDonald, British poet-novelist who died in 1905, wrote:

"To be trusted is a greater compliment than to be loved."[2]

Another Britisher, Alfred Sutro, dramatist, penned:

"Though men may not like me, they always trust my word."[3]

One American who was both trusted and loved was a man who came out of the Civil War a hero even though as commander of the Confederate Army he lost: Robert Edward Lee.

A well-groomed, brilliant, handsome leader of dignity, Lee loved the Lord, duty, and learning.

It is said that the great Confederate general, Thomas Jonathan (Stonewall) Jackson so trusted Lee that "he would follow him into battle blindfolded."[4]

After the war, Lee turned down lucrative offers and accepted the position of president for Washington College. (On his death, it was renamed Washington and Lee University.)

At the college, Lee's aide on a daily basis for three years was Edward Clifton Gordon, a Civil War veteran, who was thirty-six years younger than the general.

Said Gordon of Lee: "He was fond of elegance of every sort; fine houses, furniture, plate, clothing, ornaments, horses, equipage. But he could and did deny himself and his family the enjoyment of such things when he did not have the money to buy them."[5]

Gordon added: "He is an epistle, written of God and designed of God to teach the people of this country that earthly success is not the criterion of merit, nor the measure of true greatness."[6]

Indeed it could be said that the people trusted in Robert E. Lee because he trusted in the Lord.

Lee's credo, wrote one biographer: "God knows what is best for us."[7]

Ecclesiastes declared: "A good name is better than precious ointment." (Ecclesiastes 7:1.)

Proverbs said it even better: "A good name is rather to be chosen than great riches." (Proverbs 22:1.)

Certainly, a good name is gained and maintained through trust. And nothing is nobler than an unsullied reputation.

Notes

1. June 17, 1985, p. 19.

2. *Marquis of Lossie*, ch. 4.

3. *A Marriage Has Been Arranged* (1909).

4. *The World Book Encyclopedia*, vol. 12 (Chicago, Ill., 1980), p. 156.

5. Flood, Charles Bracelon, *Lee—The Last Years* (Boston, Mass., Houghton Mifflin Company, 1981), p. 213.

6. *Ibid.*, pp. 213–14.

7. Connelly, Thomas L., *The Marble Man* (New York, N.Y., Alfred A. Knoph, 1977), p. 191.

69

"It Seemed
a Heaven"

This was a summer Sabbath in Bellevue, Washington, beautifully cloaked with evergreen forests and flowered with pink rhododendrons.

In the Bellevue Ninth Ward sacrament meeting a comely, black-haired, brown-eyed wisp of a woman in her mid-thirties was speaking.

"I am sorry my English is not very well," she began. Her name: Saroewn Eav (pronounced *Eve*).

This was July 22, 1984.

Five years before, she and her school teacher husband, Leang Eav, had fled their home in Battambang, Cambodia. With them were a son, six; a daughter, three; and a bicycle.

Cambodia, with its ancient Buddhist treasures, for years had been torn by war.

In 1979 armed forces, both local and from neighboring Viet Nam, had overthrown the Khmer Rouge, who had ruled Cambodia for four years.

For two days the little family of four had scurried with their bicycle through the jungle to the Thai border.

For eighteen months afterward they had camped with other refugees on the border.

In 1981, shortly after their arrival in Bellevue, the Eavs joined the Church.

Now in sacrament meeting, Saroewn Eav was describing her first entry two days before into a temple: nearby Seattle Temple, spired and elegantly faced with white marble cast stone.

She told how she and her husband had for three months attended a temple preparation class: "I so surprised and scared," she said of entering the House of the Lord. "All things inside looked wonderful. It seemed a heaven."

She told how she and her husband were sealed in the temple, and how their four children were sealed to them.

Her husband, now employed at the big Boeing airplane works in Seattle, also described his feelings in that first temple exper- ience: "My new life became on Friday night (the evening they first entered the temple)," he said movingly. "The temple . . . is a place to learn of the spiritual things of God."

He, Leang Eav, has since been ordained a bishop.

Soul-lifting stories like that of the Eavs continue to happen in the temples of the Church, from Tahiti and Tonga to Taiwan and Tokyo and from São Paulo and Santiago to St. George and Salt Lake City.

Six new temples were dedicated in 1983; six more, in 1984.

In 1985 more new temples are scheduled to be dedicated than in any other year in the history of the Church: seven, as many as were dedicated in the first ninety years of the restored Church. In addition, one renovated temple, in Manti, Utah, is scheduled to be rededicated.

New temples planned to open this year circle the globe: Lima, Peru; Seoul, Korea; Chicago, Illinois; Johannesburg, South Africa; Freiberg, German Democratic Republic; Stockholm, Sweden; and Beunos Aires, Argentina.

In these edifices, sacred ordinances will be performed for both living and dead—adding to more than 250 million ordinances already completed.

More lives, like the Eavs', will be lifted heavenward.

There will be youth such as brown-eyed Heather Jensen, an A student, of Lewisburg, West Virginia. She recently asked as a twelfth birthday gift for a trip to the Washington Temple to perform baptisms for the dead. "It gives me a good feeling to know I am helping Heavenly Father and a whole bunch of other people too," wrote Heather.

And there will be more joyful temple goers like slim William B. Blair, a young adult quadriplegic of Peoria, Arizona. His home teacher, David Leake, and bishop, Don J. Lamb, take him on a bed in the bishop's van (almost an hour drive) to the Arizona Temple in Mesa. "I want to go to the temple as often as I can get a ride," smiles Bill Blair, who participates in a wheelchair.

With the new dedications, there will be hundreds added to the approximately twenty-two thousand faithful, white-clothed temple workers serving happily without pay.

Among them is Rhoda Torsak, seventy-five, a retired Bremerton, Washington school teacher. For four years twice a week she has driven 150 miles (round trip) in her car that continues to run well after some 400,000 miles—to serve in the Seattle Temple.

Also among them are Arthur D., ninety-two, and Alice E. Amner, eighty-three, converts to the Church some twenty years ago and workers in the Washington Temple for ten years. He has performed over 3,800 proxy endowments; she, over 3,000.

"It seemed a heaven," exulted a young Cambodian mother on entering the House of the Lord.

More and more faithful Latter-day Saints seem to feel that way the more they go to more temples around the world.

Index